Mary Gray-Reeves was ordained Bishop of the Episcopal Dio...
El Camino Real, located on the central Coast of California, in 2007.
Before ordination as a bishop, she served on the bishop's staff in the
Diocese of Southeast Florida and, before that, was a rector in Miami.
This is her first publication. She is intrigued by the relationship
between Church and culture and seeks to find new and effective ways
to share the good news of Jesus Christ in a rapidly changing world.

Michael Perham has been Bishop of Gloucester since 2004, and before
that was Dean of Derby. He was one of the architects of the Church
of England's *Common Worship*, and has written widely on liturgy,
theology and spirituality. He is European Bishop Protector of the
Society of St Francis and Chair of the Governing Body of both SPCK
and Ripon College Cuddesdon, UK.

THE HOSPITALITY OF GOD

Emerging Worship for a Missional Church

Mary Gray-Reeves and Michael Perham

Seabury Books
NEW YORK

Published in Great Britain in 2011 by
Society for Promoting Christian Knowledge
36 Causton Street
London SW1P 4ST
www.spckpublishing.co.uk

and in the United States of America and Canada in 2011 by
Seabury Books
445 Fifth Avenue
New York, NY 10016
www.churchpublishing.org
Seabury Books is an imprint of Church Publishing Incorporated.

British Library Cataloguing-in-Publication Data
A catalogue record for this book is available from the British Library

SPCK ISBN 978-0-281-06350-5

Library of Congress Cataloging-in-Publication Data

Gray-Reeves, Mary.
  The Hospitality of God : emerging worship for a missional church / Mary
Gray-Reeves, Michael Perham.
    p. cm.
  ISBN 978-1-59627-138-8 (e-book) – ISBN 978-1-59627-140-1 (pbk.)   1. Church
of England–Liturgy, Experimental.   2. Episcopal Church–Liturgy, Experimental.
3. Emerging church movement.   I. Perham, Michael.   II. Title.

  BX5141.G73 2011
  264′.03–dc22

2010045806

Typeset by Graphicraft Ltd, Hong Kong
Printed in the United States of America

The Hospitality of God
*is dedicated with gratitude
to the pioneering Christian leaders
creating emergent communities
and fresh expressions of church*

Contents

Acknowledgements

———•◦•◦•◦———

We express our grateful thanks to all who have made this book possible – to the many in the dioceses of El Camino Real and Gloucester and beyond who have encouraged us, to the leaders of emergent churches in the United States and of fresh expressions in England who welcomed us and gave us generously of their time and attention, to our spouses, Michael and Alison, and our work colleagues who gave us space to research, talk together and write, and to Joanna Moriarty, Publishing Director of SPCK, who warmed to the idea of this book from its inception.

+*Mary Gray-Reeves*
+*Michael Perham*

1

A pilgrimage of grace

The creation of this book has been a journey of discovery. What might have been a series of tiring journeys up and down England and across America turned out to be more like a pilgrimage of grace. This book requires rather more of an introduction and explanation than some. How has it come to be written? This chapter, by way of a preface, different in style and content from the others, sets the scene and describes the process.

The story begins at the Lambeth Conference in Canterbury in July 2008. Three bishops, Mary Gray-Reeves, Bishop of El Camino Real in California, Gerard Mpango, Bishop of Western Tanganyika in Tanzania, and Michael Perham, Bishop of Gloucester in England, sat down together and agreed to invite their dioceses to form a three-way 'companion relationship', a partnership that would work intentionally for the holding together of the Anglican Communion, by deepening friendships that would enable people to live together with difference, sometimes profoundly challenging difference, and not to walk away from one another. Through the autumn of that year negotiation by email produced an agreement and the partnership came into being on the First Sunday of Advent 2008. During the following year teams, led in each case by the bishop, visited each other's dioceses. There was a lot of prayer, worship, Bible study, attention to context, food, conversation and friendship. And the God of surprises was at work.

The nature of that partnership is still emerging and developing. We believe we have found a way of relating that other groups of dioceses might follow. We are learning how to model that mix of honesty, openness, challenge, patience, hope, trust and affection that allows us to flourish with integrity in our diversity. The unity of the Anglican Communion remains one of our primary partnership objectives, as this worldwide diverse body seeks to negotiate – intact – the all-encompassing social, political, economic and religious changes of the world.

Because of our approach to the partnership, which is designed to be in tune with the deep Christian tradition of generosity amid diversity, we have been able to witness God generously enriching our common life, beyond our expectations, enabling us to learn from one another; not least in seeing our own contexts and cultures more clearly for having been open to the contexts and cultures of others. For the teams from El Camino Real and Gloucester, making their first visit to Western Tanganyika, there was the transformative experience of living for a few days in a church where some of the challenges of the modern world, let alone the postmodern world, have not yet had to be faced, rejoicing in its vibrancy, deeply affected by its poverty, energized by its faith and its growth, made more fully aware of how the church is flourishing in Africa, even, in Tanzania, alongside and with respectful coexistence with its Muslim neighbours. For those teams to return home to California and to England was to experience also the contrast between that African confidence and the failure of the churches in the West to reach a postmodern generation that has very little know-ledge of the gospel of Jesus Christ or the life of the Church. So, not only the idea for this book but also the collaborative way of working would not have been realized without our triad partnership. The friendship and conversation of its bishops has included this area of engagement with those seeking to tell the good news afresh to a new generation, wanting to see what might be learned from what in the UK have been called 'fresh expressions of church' and in the United States 'emergence churches'. Indeed the culture of the church speaks a different language from that of secular society; and a partnership of sorts needs to be formed if we are going to communicate effect-ively. This book is born, therefore, of the collaboration of difference: not only cultural, but Michael bringing his knowledge, expertise and gifts for liturgy, Mary offering insights of one highly engaged in issues of culture, both with a passion for good worship and effective mission.

True to emergent form, the churches we visited demonstrated a disciplined ability to live with diversity, content to reach differing conclusions about any number of issues, yet united in worship; and for sacramental communities, united in the Eucharist itself. We found leaders of emergent churches highly collaborative, modelling some-thing of the way our changing world now must work; not everyone to their own preference, but rather finding common ground where diversity is not just tolerated, but understood as normative and not cause for alarm. Ultimately, of course, at the heart of all emergent churches is a deep desire to be in communion with those seeking God in Christ, receiving people as they come and journeying with them in the life of faith, allowing God's new creation to emerge. In the midst of this work, diversity just *is*.

As relationships are created anew, so is the language that seeks to reflect the new reality. At the time of this writing, the evolving language within the movement included an understanding that *emergence* was a word used to communicate the movement as a whole; that is, such as the word Protestant reflects inclusion of many denominations and a particular way of being church in Christendom. *Emergent* currently tends to reflect churches inclusive in character of all sorts and conditions of people; *emerging* is more representative of churches that are evangelical and conservative in nature. Other descriptive words associated with the movement include Deep Church, Missional Church, Neo-Monastic Church, Hyphenated, Progressive, and others. As the world is changing at a rapid speed, so is the language that attempts to give definition and voice to the massive shifts occurring in every aspect of postmodern Western life. We encourage our readers to resist the urge to become too attached to any one descriptor (because it is likely to change), but rather to increase understanding of our changing world, and discover how the timeless message of Jesus Christ – the one who was, who is and is to come – might be proclaimed in this age.

To that end and because we must use words to write a book, instead of using the double phrase 'fresh expressions/emergent church' over and over again, we have used 'emergent church' most of the time. Readers need to understand that by 'emergent church' we mean that phenomenon in the United States and the 'fresh expressions' movement in the United Kingdom. Because, as is explained below, we focused principally on Anglican and sacramental emerging churches, we did not much encounter the subtly different concept of the 'emerging' church of American evangelicalism.

That said, the intention all along was, at the end of the day, to have written a book that would be, first of all, descriptive. In general, people in the wider Church know very little about the emergent churches, and what they do know, or think they know, can make them cautious or even suspicious. Some stories need to be told and some remarkable communities described, and this book seeks to do that. But, second, there were two questions to be addressed. One of them turned out to be simple to answer: 'What might the emergent churches learn from the church's liturgical tradition if they were open to it?' This book will develop the answer, but essentially it is this. Of course there is endless resource in the tradition. But the emergent churches are very open to it, perhaps more open than the inherited church. There is no reluctance among emerging churches to search the tradition and to re-energize it.

The other question is more complex: 'What might the inherited church learn from the worship of the emergent churches?' The greater part of this book is devoted to that. There are some easy lessons to learn, recovering some lost arts, investing some ancient forms with new energy, taking some risks. There are also some difficult issues, where to listen to the emergent churches would challenge, at quite a fundamental level, some of the assumptions and the rules of liturgical life in the inherited church. The church needs to begin a dialogue of sorts between itself as institution and its essence as the body of God's salvation, called to proclaim and include all who seek to be part of Jesus Christ, especially those who have no knowledge or understanding of this sacred story.

We needed to set clear parameters to the subject. We clarified for ourselves that we were not looking at alternative services in inherited churches. Clearly many inherited churches that do not think of themselves as 'emergent' are nevertheless becoming open to alternative worship of various kinds. But to have included these would have been far too broad a subject for us to tackle. We wanted to engage with the worship of new churches and of communities which, if they had begun their life within the inherited church, had moved into sufficiently new territory to be emergent churches. In general we stayed with that principle, though we were helped by two powerful experiences in Seattle from within the inherited church that are described in Chapter 6 and in Worshipping communities 4 (page 79).

We further clarified that what we were exploring was the worship within these communities. We were not uninterested in other aspects of their life, the extent to which, for instance, they saw themselves as 'missional' communities. Indeed that is, in some ways, more fundamental than anything else to their flourishing. Nor were we focusing on their pastoral care – of their own members or of the wider communities in which they were set – nor on their teaching/learning opportunities outside a liturgical context. Our attention was on their worship. Inevitably that drew us into related questions, about how they understood community, authority and accountability. We have not avoided these issues, but the worship remains the focus.

There have been two more clarifications. The first has been that we have restricted ourselves to emergent churches that see themselves as Anglican, whether through the Church of England or in the United States through The Episcopal Church. All but two of the churches that we visited were led by an episcopally authorized minister. Of the other two, one was led by a Methodist minister, and even that church was jointly sponsored by the local Anglican diocese. The other sat light to accountability with its diocese, though its leaders had strong roots in The Episcopal Church.

The second has been that we have concentrated on emerging churches where words like 'catholic', 'sacramental', 'eucharistic' and 'contemplative' have rung bells. Nine of the 14 communities we write about in this book were celebrating the Eucharist on the day we visited them.

So, in short, this study explores worship in Anglican emergent churches in the sacramental tradition on both sides of the Atlantic, seeking to reveal the liturgical life that unites emergent and inherited churches alike and searching for lessons and insights for all communities, inherited or emerging, that understand themselves to be Anglican, sacramental and open to where the Holy Spirit might lead in the renewal of worship. We would not want to claim that conclusions can be drawn about the emerging church movement in its widest sense from what we saw. Clearly there are other forms of fresh expression, outside the sacramental tradition, about which very different conclusions could be drawn.

Of the 14 communities visited, seven were in England and Michael Perham alone went to share in their worship. These were Sanctus1 in Manchester, Home in Oxford, Ethos @ St Nick's in Portsmouth, Transcendence in York, Safe Space in Telford, Blesséd in Gosport and Moot in London. He also had conversations with Richard White about Dream in Liverpool, with Jonny Baker about Grace in London and with Michael Volland about Feig in his own diocese of Gloucester. In the middle of the English tour came two weeks in the United States, where he and Mary Gray-Reeves together shared in worship with Transmission in New York, at The Crossing in Boston, at St Gregory of Nyssa in San Francisco, at St Paul's Church, the Church of the Apostles and St Mark's Cathedral in Seattle, and at Thad's in Los Angeles.

We should record here that these 14 communities where we worshipped are very diverse. We worshipped in a Manhattan apartment. We were caught up in the liturgy in cathedrals. We celebrated the Eucharist and received consecrated bread and wine. We were drawn into new rituals with ash and with stones. Most of the communities who welcomed us would describe themselves as 'emergent churches' or 'fresh expressions of church', but three did not exactly fit that model. St Gregory of Nyssa in San Francisco, although it exhibits many of the characteristics of the emerging churches, predated the emerging church movement by several years, having been founded in 1978. The service of Compline in St Mark's Cathedral in Seattle, for all its attraction to what is sometimes called Generation Y or 'Gen Y' (those born from the 1980s), is a deeply meditative liturgical form; to share in it felt like participation in the worship of an emergent church community. St Paul's Church in Seattle regards itself as a 'progressive Anglo-Catholic church', and though it has its own alternative worship the service we attended was in no way alternative, but a deeply spiritual eucharistic celebration of the inherited church. We have included it in order to have a good model of mainstream liturgical life to set alongside what is developing in the emerging churches. 'Anglo-Catholic' in the United States, it should be noted, has a different ring to it from how the term is used in England. In England it has been almost entirely captured by those opposed to the ordination of women. At St Paul's the rector is a woman and the community is inclusive, exemplifying that such a characterization is not typical in the American expression of Anglicanism.

In each of our visits the method was to share in worship, and to be, as far as possible, worshippers, rather than observers, very rarely writing anything down during the worship, but participating fully. Afterwards (or sometimes before) there were long conversations with the leaders of each community, who were generous with their time and open and honest, as well as motivated and enthusiastic, about their communities and their worship. Everything was then recorded in some detail – a general description of the church and its life, a detailed description of the liturgy in which we shared, some reflections on the experience, and a record of the conversation with the leaders.

Where we went together to visit a community in the United States, we talked much together, questioning, making connections, modifying each other's insights. There was a lot of animated conversation!

We employed a similar approach with the material from the communities in England. Although it was Michael alone who visited them, we have so pored over the reports together that they too feel like co-authored work. It is for this reason that we have felt able to use the plural 'we' throughout the following chapters. We have worked together sufficiently on this material for us both to own the whole experience and the conclusions that are drawn. Furthermore it is true that emergent communities in both countries collaborate, demonstrate similar worship trends and processes of reflection, making our own collaboration relatively easy.

Some of the material in those 14 accounts has found its way, almost unedited, into this book. The majority of it formed the raw material for the conversations reflected in the book.

The different cultural contexts of our two churches and the nations within which they minister have meant that there have inevitably been moments when finding the right word or phrase has been difficult, with the danger that we might be misunderstood in either an English or an American context. We have tried quite hard to express things in a way that will communicate clearly on both sides of the Atlantic, and where we have been aware of significant differences of language and culture, to signal those differences. On a few occasions we have struggled; despite a common language and shared admiration for what the emergent churches are modelling, there were moments when reaching agreement on what to say tested our determination to produce an agreed text, but that is what we have achieved. We have learned a lot about each other's mind. Working patiently to understand the other's mind is, of course, what is desperately needed, not only in relationships between the inherited and emergent churches, but between Anglicans in different cultures.

In passing, it is worth noting that the way this book has been written, drawing on our common experience and the material we wrote together, but then refining with drafts going from one to the other by email and editing conversations by skype, is itself an expression of a new way of working that is part of the fast-changing culture in which the church seeks to minister.

Of the 14 churches where we worshipped, we have provided here detailed descriptions of six, in order to give our readers the flavour of the places we have visited and real insight into their worshipping life. This does not mean that these six are more interesting or important than the others, which do not have a whole section of their own but feature instead through references throughout the book. Every one of the 14 taught us something. Some of them moved us deeply and touched our souls.

The shape of the book is that the 12 chapters have interleaved between them either (in six cases) the account of a particular church community or (in five cases) some striking liturgical texts we met on our travels, texts created in a particular community for that community. They show something of the quality of writing within these churches and also the theology the communities want to embrace and share.

The title of this book, *The Hospitality of God*, reflects what has seemed to us to be a major emphasis of the emergent churches, laying stress on God's desire to be welcoming, hospitable, inclusive, inviting. For ourselves, wherever we went we encountered something of that unconditional hospitality, reflected in the communities and especially in their leaders, giving of themselves generously to us. We found them to be deeply impressive Christian ministers, of high intellectual calibre and mature faith and spirituality: pioneering adventurers, whom the church should honour.

But alongside the hospitality we sensed the spirit of pilgrimage. In that spirit, it was clear that emergent churches were most interested not in the political divisions of the Anglican Communion but rather in embarking upon a journey of creating a collaborative conversation between faith in Jesus Christ and the secular culture in which we live today. In this sense, we found emergent churches prophetic to the institutional church: demonstratively inclusive of those who do not know Jesus, able to readily hear and converse with their experience, participating in the making of a new creation, a new church, born of a relationship between faith and the local context of the world in which we live. Here were people on a journey, uncertain in many cases where it was God wanted these churches ultimately to be, but confident that Jesus was with them on the journey, was blessing them through the events of the journey and would bring something good, exciting and renewing for the whole Church out of the adventure in which they were engaged. We caught something of that spirit, so that far from tiresome journeys on motorways or aeroplanes we found ourselves on a pilgrimage, one in which we experienced many moments of grace, bringing us to a new place, more capable of proclaiming good news in this new age.

Worshipping communities 1: Transcendence

York – 14 February 2010

Transcendence is an offshoot of Visions, a fresh expressions community that has existed in York since 1992, though there were some years of germination before that within the St Michael le Belfry Church community. The Visions community, which meets weekly in St Cuthbert's Church, numbers about 20 and has done so throughout its existence. Its leader until the summer of 2010 was Sue Wallace, who has been involved since the beginning and, after theological training at Mirfield, was ordained in 2006. She has been supported financially by the community.

Transcendence was begun in 2007. While St Cuthbert's was undergoing renovation, Visions made use of the crypt of York Minster. Building on that and identifying a gap, Transcendence was born as a series of alternative worship events that took seriously the building, spirituality and liturgical style of the Minster. Sue was the lead-player in this, but working with Jeremy Fletcher, then the Precentor of the Minster.

Transcendence happens in the Minster once a month on a Sunday at 7.30 p.m., normally in the Chapter House but usually breaking out into other parts of the building at some points during the worship. There were about 150 people present on 14 February, and that is apparently typical, with a wide age range, children through to very senior citizens. Most had the look of people used to sharing in liturgy. Most, we suspected, had other church allegiances.

Sue has had some hope of there being a Transcendence community, but at present it remains an event generated by Visions. It may well be that Transcendence is too big and public to be a fresh expression of church and will remain an alternative worship event parented by both Visions and the Minster community.

This was in many ways traditional catholic liturgy. All the signs of catholic liturgy were visible – altar, three ministers in vestments, candles, Book of the Gospels, incense, well-choreographed ceremonial. The Gospel procession, described in Chapter 5, from the Chapter House into the main church was a beautiful corporate experience. If it was a fresh expression of worship, it was one that drew deeply on the tradition. There were novel elements, of course: icons and two screens for projected words and images. Musically and visually it was very different from an old-fashioned High Mass, and seating was in the round and on chairs, with some beanbags. But what made it effective were not the novel elements, but the sheer love, energy and gentle confidence that went into the entire celebration.

There seemed to be so much that had gone into it that we wondered whether it would be sustainable on a weekly basis. Is what makes liturgy in many churches flat the sheer hard work of producing something that refreshes the tradition every single week? Sue thought not. The music and the visuals, where most of the work would appear to be required, are not created *ex nihilo* each time, but rather there is a huge bank of material that has been built up over the years and can be reused.

The question, of course, is whether a great liturgical event, with a crowd of people, can turn into an emergent church. There must be circumstances in which it can, but Transcendence does not seem to be of the kind that will. It will go on being a powerful event and it may indeed be for some people the one setting in which they experience church, but it will not be a community. It will be one of the Minster's congregations, probably the one with the widest age range and greatest vitality, inspired and enabled by the Visions community, and that is a very good thing to be.

2

Revisiting Anglican principles

There is a widespread suspicion in the inherited church that the emergent churches within Anglicanism do not take canon law in relation to worship, or indeed the whole ethos of Anglican liturgy, seriously. We found that there were some quite important areas where the emergent churches are at variance with the rest of the church, but the overall picture was, to our mind, one where, consciously or unconsciously, emerging church leaders and congregations were working very much with the flow of Anglican liturgical principle and practice.

In this chapter we have set out 20 such principles. They are not an official set of rules, approved by any province, but they will be accepted by Anglicans both in the UK and in the United States as ways in which Anglican worship can be recognized. Many of them are not, of course, unique to Anglicanism, and not every one of them would be embraced by all Anglicans. But together they build up a picture that is faithful to our tradition. In each case we have recorded very briefly how the emergent churches seem to respond to the principle. In Chapters 4 to 10 we expand those responses in greater detail and with stories of particular communities. At the end of this chapter we add five principles that, though not exclusive to the emergent churches, seem to have prominence and emphasis there.

1 Liturgy is ordered with beauty and holiness to reflect the beauty and holiness of God

With its continuity with the Catholic Church of pre-Reformation days, Anglicanism has always had a concern for worship that is aesthetically pleasing, a beautiful offering to God of all the best that humankind can create. From the time of Archbishop William Laud in the seventeenth century, the phrase from the Book of Psalms, 'the beauty of holiness' (Psalm 96.9, AV), has had a particular appeal to Anglicans, and with it there has always been an implication that the other side of the same coin is 'the holiness of beauty'. Carefully crafted words and careful but unfussy movement and gesture, influenced in England by the Benedictine tradition, have been important to us.

Nearly all the emergent churches buy into this principle. None are dismissive of beauty. Some attach huge importance to it and invest much time and energy in trying to create it. In many emergent churches all the senses are fully involved in worship.

2 Liturgy is the normal way Anglicans worship God together

Traditionally Anglicans have offered their worship within the framework of the Book of Common Prayer, with the Church of England looking back to the Prayer Book of 1662 and The Episcopal Church to the Scottish Prayer Book of 1637 and to the American Prayer Book of 1979. Subsequent revisions have loosened up the liturgy, encouraging greater variation and spontaneity, but always within a liturgical context, in which shape, word, song, movement, gesture and silence all have their place. Especially in England recent decades have seen some churches, mainly in an evangelical tradition, move away from a liturgical norm, but in general Anglicans have continued to work within the broad constraints of the liturgy.

There are some emergent churches that sit light to liturgy, but the ones we visited rated it highly. The view generally is that even some of the more evangelical emerging churches come to appreciate the need for liturgy. There is a post-evangelical rediscovery of the power of liturgy.

3 A degree of commonality in liturgy is needed to maintain and enhance the unity of the Church

Part of how Anglicans recognize their family likeness one with another is through their liturgical coherence. This is not a straitjacket, either within a particular province or between provinces, but there are sufficient common texts and shared styles, a distinctive ethos – sometimes more recognizable to people from other Christian traditions than to those within the Communion – and that is part of what holds the Church together. This is unsurprising in a Communion that used to look to a shared prayer book as a source of unity.

Most emergent churches have some appreciation of commonality. Some use recognized and authorized liturgical texts, a few nothing but authorized texts. Some use no common texts but value common shape. Most are in touch with one another and use each other's resources.

4 The Christian formation of the people of God individually and as community takes place within the celebration of the liturgy

This, for most Anglicans, is both self-evident and also unconscious. People have not come to church in order to be formed or transformed, but it happens, simply because that is how liturgy, repeated week in week out, touches at the deepest level and penetrates the soul. In the contemporary church people have become more conscious of this truth, and speak, in a new way, about the liturgy as formational and transformational. In terms of how the community is formed and re-formed, it is true that the liturgy both shapes the Church and reflects the Church, acting out in the liturgical context all that Paul teaches about the body with its different parts, its gifts and its ministries.

Emergent churches recognize the power of liturgy and take it very seriously. For some of them the worship is the one and only formational gathering. The intentional focused participation in the liturgy suggests a desire to grow and be formed through it.

5 Our doctrine is derived from our liturgy (*lex orandi, lex credendi*)

Because we have never been a confessional church, it is to our liturgy that we turn (and to which we point others) to discover what our faith is, both what we share with all Christians and what is distinctive to our tradition. The old Latin adage, *lex orandi, lex credendi*, affirms that what we believe is what we pray. It is this, of course, that accounts for our insistence, one that would seem strange to many traditions, on our key liturgical texts being subjected to scrutiny in synods and conventions and especially by the House of Bishops. Because the liturgical texts define doctrine, and even the liturgical rubrics can imply doctrine, they need authorization, lest we change our doctrine almost without realizing it.

Emergent churches will recognize that it is what people do and say liturgically that will shape their belief. Some of them will be clear that the liturgy should be offering the 'faith of the Church' and these will probably use authorized texts (especially for the Eucharistic Prayer with its rehearsing of the story of salvation) frequently. Others will feel a freedom to create their own texts and to push at the boundaries of 'orthodoxy'. Most will want texts to be presented in such a way that assent is not demanded. Some emergent churches would shrink from any thought that texts needed 'authorizing' by a church authority.

6 Scripture, both as lection and as song (psalms and canticles), is always present in our liturgy and we read it in step with one another through the use of common lectionaries

Anglicans, through their highly scriptural daily office, where not only are the lections from the Bible but much of the prayer and praise is in the form of psalms and canticles, have always kept the Scriptures at the heart of worship. The use across much of the Communion of the Revised Common Lectionary has led to a broader experience of Scripture by members of congregations and to a greater experience of unity (reaching beyond the Communion) as we read and explore the same Scriptures together. Although there is little desire to enforce conformity to lectionaries, and some parishes devise their own, there is a general recognition that the use of the lectionary both keeps the Communion together and ensures that a breadth of Scripture is heard.

The emergent churches we visited took Scripture very seriously. The majority followed the lectionary, several used all three readings, most enabled people to explore the readings further during 'Open Space' or 'Stations', some sang the Gospel. Psalmody was employed more than one might have expected. Many of the songs in use are versions of psalms or other passages of Scripture. Some spoke of the reading of the Scriptures as 'the word of the Lord'.

7 Anglicans use some texts sufficiently frequently that they enter the memory and feed the soul

It is, of course, the words that people actually use over and over again that enter their memory and their soul. These are not necessarily the foundational texts to which the scholars (or in England the Declaration of Assent) draw us back. The texts that shape people's beliefs are those, often contemporary ones, that people use the most. People have come to recognize that if every time you hear a text it is in a different translation, or if every time you come to worship you use freshly composed texts you have not heard before and may not hear again, your memory bank account will be almost empty. That may not matter at some stages in your life, but at some point that loss will impoverish your spirituality.

It is, of course, texts that are sung that most easily slip into the memory and most emerging churches sing a good deal, though not always the words of the authorized liturgy itself. Feeding the long-term memory is not an obvious concern of emergent churches any more than it is of most young people. St Gregory of Nyssa in San Francisco (which is not a congregation particularly targeted to those born since the 1960s) is a major exception, with a liturgy based on frequent repetition of familiar texts.

8 Liturgy normally includes prayers of thanksgiving, penitence and intercession, some prayers in 'collect' form, creed and blessing, and principal services include a sermon

Anglican worship traditionally includes these elements on most occasions. Foundational forms of Morning and Evening Prayer include thanksgiving, penitence, intercession, creed and collect, as do contemporary forms of the Eucharist. Most services end with blessing. Although only at the Eucharist is the preaching of a sermon prescribed, most Anglicans expect to hear one at any principal service on a Sunday.

Here emergent churches differ a good deal from one another. Thanksgiving is present in every church that celebrates the Eucharist, as most do. Penitence, however, is an area where we encountered real diversity. Some, clearly, rarely used prayers of confession, others included them during Lent, while some would have them on each occasion simply because they formed part of an authorized order. The use of an absolution was rare.

Intercession also revealed variety. Some had 'the prayers of the people', and if they did so it was almost always with opportunity for anyone to speak into the prayers. One community had intercession in the Eucharistic Prayer. Some encouraged intercessory prayer within the Open Space stations. Some seemed to include no intercessory element, and felt self-absorbed, with the needs of the world not on their agenda.

The collect form, which has a prominent place in Anglicanism, was employed mainly through the use of authorized texts, but not widely.

Emergent churches do not much use creeds. In the emergent churches we visited we experienced the saying of the Creed by the congregation only once and then with some altered text. In St Mark's Episcopal Cathedral in Seattle we saw more than 500 young people stand reverently and silently while it was recited, although St Mark's does not characterize this service as emergent.

Most of the churches included a blessing and dismissal.

Some included a sermon/homily, and some indicated that they varied their practice. In some the homily was 'unpacked' in discussion together. The churches that had Open Space or Stations mainly saw this as an opportunity to engage with either the readings (making it a kind of privatized sermon/homily to oneself) or with the preached homily.

9 Liturgy is dialogue

Unlike some traditions where the congregation does not make acclamations, enter formal liturgical dialogue with the leaders of worship or speak prayers together, Anglicans have normally done all these things and never restricted their oral participation to the occasional 'Amen' and the singing of the hymns and songs.

Here there is huge variety in emergent churches, from communities where there is no dialogue or spoken prayer to others where much of the liturgy is a dialogue between minister (presider or deacon) and people. In general more of their prayers were spoken together (less of ministers speaking alone, speaking together probably being seen as more collaborative/participatory than listening to the single voice of the leader). Sometimes there was an antiphonal approach, with two alternating sets of voices.

10 In any liturgy there is usually a reference to the Trinity, prayers are offered through Jesus and the Spirit invoked

The Trinitarian emphasis in Anglican worship is not over-laboured, but the use of 'In the name of the Father . . .' is frequent, as is the saying of 'The grace of our Lord Jesus Christ . . .'; collects often, and the Eucharistic Prayers always, are drawn together in a Trinitarian doxology. Prayers are almost always offered 'through Jesus Christ our Lord'. The calling down of the Spirit at Baptism and the Eucharist is fairly fundamental. Even the 1662 Communion rite, which has no *epiclesis* (prayer for the action of the Spirit) in the Prayer of Consecration, prays at the beginning of the rite for God to 'cleanse the thoughts of our hearts by the inspiration of thy Holy Spirit'.

Although not every emergent church uses authorized texts, the prayers we have encountered have not been strikingly different from those in mainstream churches. There has not been a great emphasis on the Trinity, but nor has the Trinity been left unmentioned. The figure of Jesus is clearly important. Few of the prayers written in the emergent churches end with the classic 'through Jesus Christ our Lord', but this may have more to do with lack of experience of writing prayer or perhaps a general dislike for established formulae than any desire to play down the place of Jesus in prayer. Where the Eucharist is celebrated there has always been an invocation of the Holy Spirit.

11 There are distinctive roles in the liturgy for the orders of the church – laity, deacons, priests and bishops

Where they had lost it, Anglicans have recovered the sense of the liturgy as 'the work of the people', with every person present a 'celebrant'; but with that there has also come a greater understanding of the particular role of the one who presides (in England called the 'president', in the United States the 'presider') and a recovery in many churches of the diaconal role.

There are some emergent churches that are distrustful of what they regard as hierarchy (which they understand as some offices/order being regarded as more important than others). The whole language of distinctive roles would be seen as unhelpful. In most of the emergent churches we visited the distinctive role of ordained ministers was respected, though there was a playing down of presidency in favour of a more collaborative low-profile leadership of worship. In most the role of lay people was developed fully in reading, leading prayer, and assisting with the distribution of the consecrated bread and wine.

12 The laity express their participation in the liturgy both by what they do together and by what individuals are called out to do as representatives of the people

Emphasis in Anglican liturgy on the representative role of the laity in the liturgy, reflecting a 'body of Christ' theology, is relatively recent (though now well established) ecclesiology, but an understanding that the deepest expression of participation is by prayerfully and attentively sharing with the community in the celebration has been an Anglican insight from the time of the first prayer books.

Emergent church communities have a strong sense of belonging one to another, of worshipping as something done together; remarkably so, considering that they contain people of widely differing theological opinions who seem able to accept one another. There is a gentle acceptance that everyone is on a slightly different spiritual journey, or at least a different stage of the journey. There is a deep sense of participation; very rarely does anyone seem detached. This expresses itself in the majority of emergent churches in a good deal of communal speaking, but more deeply one senses real spiritual communion in these gatherings. In eucharistic communities this seems centred in the incarnation; in the body and blood of Christ at the table. Even in non-eucharistic gatherings and churches where there is more listening than speaking (as at Compline at St Mark's Cathedral in Seattle) one could still sense this deep participation. It is also noteworthy that there is almost more interest in sharing in the devising of the liturgy than having a role within its celebration.

13 Liturgy is normally led by ministers ordained or authorized by the bishop and the president of the Eucharist is always a priest or a bishop

Although there are voices within the Anglican Communion calling for lay celebration, the presidency of the Eucharist by a bishop or a priest is absolutely fundamental in the ecclesiology of both The Episcopal Church and the Church of England. Beyond that, although there has been a loosening of rules and more leadership of non-sacramental worship by people without specific episcopal authorization, the culture of our churches is still to expect those who lead main services or who preach at them to be ordained or, if not ordained, licensed by the bishop.

Although there are, of course, a number of emergent churches that are not in relationship with the local bishop, all but one of the churches we visited were in such a relationship. In all of them except two, both meeting in private homes, the Eucharist always has a priest as eucharistic president. Preaching was usually, though not exclusively, done by the ordained.

14 Liturgical shape is more fundamental than liturgical text

This is not a long-standing insight of Anglican liturgy, which in the past has been very controlled by prayer books with authorized texts and tight rubrics. But every recent revision has introduced more freedom and variety and both the 1979 American Book of Common Prayer and the 2000 English *Common Worship* have included an order for the Eucharist, prescribing shape, but no text.

On this all emergent churches would be agreed. Few feel bound by authorized texts, but we were struck by how conventional most have been in their shaping of worship.

15 Movement and gesture are not over-prescribed, but normally have place in the liturgy

Issues relating to 'ceremonial' have, in the Anglican tradition, been more a matter of custom than law, apart from some prescriptive canons and rubrics. Styles have varied, reflecting different approaches to both liturgical tradition and theology, and have changed over the years, in response to fresh thinking and, to some extent, liturgical fashion. The most striking example of this has been the variety in the position the presiding minister occupies in relation to the altar table. But, however much these concerns have been a matter of local custom, very few churches attach no importance to such issues, and some of the changes, such as the moving of the altar table from the wall to allow people to gather around it, have been highly significant. Most churches are clear as to what they do, though not always why they do it.

In general, emergent churches warm to ceremonial, processional movements, clear gestures by the leaders and in some cases by the entire congregation, and have a very firm understanding of what they are doing and of the history that lies behind it. In some cases congregational shared gestures replaced congregational shared words. In one church we encountered a congregation where everyone acted together in harmony in terms of ritual gesture in a way that felt deeply engaged and uniting.

16 Liturgy usually includes music: Anglicans value hymnody, sing Scripture as well as read it and recognize that music deepens the experience of worship

From the earliest prayer books there has been provision for texts to be sung and mention made of anthems. Hymnody came later. In England no particular hymn book has authority, but in the United States The Episcopal Church approves *The Hymnal* as well as the Prayer Book, though the choice of hymns and songs is not limited to those books.

Whereas in many evangelical and Protestant churches the tendency is to sing the hymns and songs and not the liturgical texts, in Anglicanism the singing of such Scriptures as the Song of Mary (the *Magnificat*) and the psalms is deeply embedded, as is the singing of the 'common' of the Eucharist – Gloria, Sanctus, for example.

Almost every emergent church values music. In some it is recorded and in some it is the prerogative of a music group, but in most there is an encouragement to sing. Some adopt a single simple musical style, perhaps emerging from a contemporary musical culture familiar to the participants, easy for the whole congregation to sing, but the majority adopt a variety of styles, drawing on the traditional and the contemporary. Instruments are important for some, but we perceived a growth in singing without accompaniment.

17 Ordained ministers and others leading worship usually wear distinctive liturgical vesture

Canon law in England requires the wearing of robes and vestments for statutory services. In The Episcopal Church there is no such canonical requirement, but the use of robes and vestments is normal. The majority of the inherited church congregations in both countries value this for a number of reasons, including continuity with the past, a sense of worship as theatre and a desire not to identify the minister by his/her choice of clothes with any particular social group. But many churches now have some services led by people not wearing distinctive robes and some churches, usually evangelical ones, have abandoned robes altogether, usually in the cause of mission. Bishops in general have not sought to impose these canons against the will of the local church.

In emergent churches there is some diversity. In one community full eucharistic vestments were worn by the three ministers. At another almost every member of the worship team wore some distinctive liturgical garment. But in the majority no distinctive garments were worn, except in some cases a stole put on over ordinary clothes (with clergy in clerical collars) just before the Eucharistic Prayer.

18 The liturgy reflects the times and seasons of the Christian year with their distinctive and contrasting moods

At the Reformation much of the celebration of the seasons of the Christian calendar was suppressed. The Prayer Book of 1662 made little seasonal provision, but through hymnody and, from the nineteenth century, through supplementary and initially unofficial texts and through such means as liturgical colours, the different shades of the Christian seasons returned. Twentieth-century liturgical renewal accentuated this return. The Church of England's *Common Worship: Times and Seasons* has brought this to a new level. Although some evangelical churches lay less emphasis on the seasons, for most Anglicans the cycle from Advent through to All Saintstide enriches the liturgy through the year.

In England our initial visits were during Ordinary Time, so there was little opportunity to reflect season, though the eucharistic celebrations followed the lectionary. In America all our visits were in Lent and every church took that theme seriously. Most increased their penitential material because it was Lent and explored Lenten themes. Some emergent churches (principally those with post-evangelical leadership) regard the recovery of the Christian year as one of the distinctive marks of their communities.

19 Canon law describes who may be invited to receive Holy Communion

Though there is some difference between The Episcopal Church and the Church of England in relation to admission to Communion before Confirmation, both are clear in canon law that Holy Communion is reserved to the baptized and only a few mainstream churches openly and explicitly deviate from that, though many others do not overemphasize or police the rules. The welcome is, at an official level, conditional.

This is the one thing on which emergent churches seem almost uniformly at odds with the tradition. They have an open table and lay much emphasis on it – *all* are welcome. The 'all' in most places includes children, however young, and the unbaptized of all ages, whether seeking initiation or with no intention of doing so. The Eucharist (belonging) is often seen as the way to Baptism (believing).

20 Anglicans feel free to draw selectively on the liturgical traditions of other communities

Ever since Thomas Cranmer drew on the Catholic liturgy, but also on the liturgical work of the continental reformers, Anglicanism has been willing to employ liturgical treasures from various sources.

The twentieth-century ecumenical movement encouraged such an approach. Any contemporary service book will include material from both East and West, Catholic and Reformed, from other Anglican provinces and from unofficial texts for which no authorization has been sought. The only constraint is that for some texts, material drawn from other traditions has to be authorized for Anglican use.

Emergent churches practise this well. Nearly all borrow texts and rituals from other churches and from one another (through a strong transatlantic network). They are also, ironically, better than many other churches at recovering the lost texts and practices deep in the tradition. There is much talk of 'ancient future'. We encountered leaders who were well studied and serious about their craft as liturgists.

To complete this overview, before exploring the elements in greater detail in the chapters that follow, we need to indicate five additional characteristics of emergent church worship.

1 Every liturgical occasion requires careful detailed planning

There is very little sense of using material written for a previous occasion. Each occasion, even when it follows a well-established shape and pattern, is a unique event, thought through and planned, usually by a group working collaboratively. Nearly always there is a target group in mind, recognizing that people unfamiliar with church need to be handled with care, that all have a desire to belong and be loved, and some may have pastoral needs that include pain experienced in an earlier phase of church membership.

2 Welcome precedes any sense of either belonging or believing

There is an intentional welcome of those who do not belong to the church, both those who once belonged at one time in their life and those who have never had any contact with organized religion. There may need to be a radical welcome that includes clear instructions, invitation and expectation, from the moment one walks through the door. Oral rubrics are necessary during the service with no expect-ation that people will know the liturgy, or, better, in order to create an atmosphere where people are put at ease and included by being swept up and carried along by a confident worshipping community.

3 The liturgy expresses indigenous authenticity

We heard consistently from emergent leaders that liturgy arises from the people rather than by strict imposition of outside criteria or tradition. Emergent churches are truly interested in, conscious of and connected to their ministry context.

4 Liturgy needs to be multi-sensory and have complexity

Emergent churches take seriously the need to employ all the senses, and especially the recovery of the visual. Worship should present a variety of options for people to express themselves and offer something forward by way of art, reflection, prayer, study or meditation. In several settings, more than one activity was offered at the same time – singing, dancing and processing, for instance – and Open Space, a series of stations that provide people with options for sermon response rather than a single route for engagement.

5 A primary aim of worship is to feed the soul

Emergent churches we visited were consistent in their desire to welcome and connect people to God, focusing on feeding the soul of the participant. This was expressed in prayers that reflected people's sense of journey, pastoral care needs and life focus, as well as in use of psalms, full inclusion in all activities, and liturgical design that set the participant at ease.

These characteristics are not exclusive to the emergent churches. They are to be found in the inherited church, but they seem to have more importance and emphasis in emergent churches, as the following chapters will testify.

Words for worship 1: Invitations

Come, all you who thirst,
all you who hunger for the bread of life,
all you whose souls cry out for healing;
Come, come to the feast of life.

Come, all you who are weary,
all you who are bowed down with worry,
all you who ache with the tiredness of living;
Come, come to the feast of life.

Come, all you poor,
all you who are without food or refuge,
all you who go hungry in a fat land;
Come, come to the feast of life.

Come, all you who are bitter,
all you whose hopes have tarnished into cynicism,
all you who feel betrayed and cannot forgive;
Come, come to the feast of life.

Come, all who grieve,
all you who suffer loss as a fresh knife wound,
all you who curse the God you love;
Come, come to the feast of life.

Come, all you who are sinners,
all you who have sold the gift that is within you,
all you who toss uneasily in your bed at night;
Come, come to the feast of life.

Come, all you who are oppressed,
all you who have forgotten the meaning of freedom,
all you whose cries cut to the very heart of God;
Come, come to the feast of life.

Come, all you who are traitors,
all you who use your wealth and power to crucify God,
all you who cannot help yourselves;
Come, come to the feast of life.

Come, all you who are sick,
all you whose bodies have failed you,
all you who long above all for healing;
Come, come to the feast of life.

Come all you who are lost,
all you who search for meaning but cannot find it,
all you who have no place of belonging;
Come, come to the feast of life.

The table of Jesus is your place of gathering.
Here you are welcomed, wanted, loved.
Here is a place set for you.
Come, come to the feast of life.

Mike Riddell

All are invited, all are included
All are made welcome, none are excluded
This is the table of Christ
Come if you're young, come if you're old
Come if you're broken, come if you're whole
Come if you're weary of the trials of life
This is the table of Christ.

Jesus the host washes your feet
Makes you his guest and lays on a feast
This is the table of Christ
Come if you're rich, come if you're poor
Come if the church stops you at the door
Come and eat bread, come and drink wine
This is the table of Christ.

Eat and remember Jesus the one
Who gave up his life so you could belong
This is the table of Christ
Come if you're thirsty, come and be filled
Come and be clean, come and be healed
Come and be held in the presence of God
This is the table of Christ.

Jonny Baker

3

Authority is a conversation

———•◆•———

As one begins to explore the emergence movement, one sees immediately the impact of the wholesale shift in society also occurring in the church. While other denominations may advocate separation from the world, Anglicanism does not. While not of the world, we are called to be in it. As we seek to expand our reach with the gospel of Jesus Christ, we must be fluent in the culture in which we live, and so cannot ignore how life is changing in unprecedented ways. We are all, to some extent, a product of our environment; a reality that is never static. Throughout history, liturgy has emerged as part of a conversation with the surrounding culture of both church and society. This chapter seeks to highlight some of the cultural shifts in how the postmodern understanding of authority has shifted, and its imminent impact on the emergent worship setting in the Anglican context.

We hear via a multitude of sources both in and outside the church that authority, and who has it, is a key point of transformation of the postmodern reality. Phyllis Tickle, in her book *The Great Emergence*, offers a summary of how developments in science and culture have helped us come to where we are and continue to influence where we are headed. While there is much to consider, it is helpful to pause for a moment just to think of the many forces of change that have emerged in the last 50 years: increased mobility, communication, and civil rights for women and minorities, to name just three that have had a tremendous effect on the day-to-day functioning of the average person in the Western world. These have also affected the church, encouraging us to consider different ways of understanding God and the human community.

Amid these shifts, liberation theologians have helped articulate the perspective of those with historically less power in both church and culture, naming them as included in God's kingdom, through the compassion and radical embrace of the life, death and resurrection of Jesus Christ. When one takes this to heart, seeking to order the church and the world accordingly, there is necessarily more intentional listening to and acting with a greater variety of people. While many in the church would like to continue in a more traditional world-view, emergent Christians (and one can see this in the mainline institution of the church as well) have discovered rich blessings from those on power's edge. They have welcomed these insights and this has transformed the way they do ministry. While some have learned new leadership strategies to engage ministry in this way, the under-40 demographic most naturally functions in this leadership style because it is their cultural make-up. The current culture converses more readily with diversity and it has shaped the hearts, minds and souls of those who dwell there.

Inherent in the make-up of change in our culture is the inclusion of women in more areas of professional life and ministry than at any point in history. For many, this has prompted reflection and change in leadership models. It is generally recognized that there are differences in how organizations function when women have a stronger presence than when functioning as a significant minority or not at all. For those of us in churches where women exercise authority in all orders of ministry, we understand that the presence of women affects the daily relational functioning of the church exponentially. Furthermore, it is simply true that women are enculturated to exercise authority differently from men, for reasons best articulated by feminist theologians, but in short in ways that tend to be more collegial, and with a posture that is more conciliatory and inclusive of the authority of others. The conscious and informed experience of women as the gender with less power in the Church, therefore, has shaped how they exercise authority; this mode is a means by which a person with less voice converses with a dominant authority when needing to be heard. Leadership by women has now effectively evolved in non-traditional ways that are theologically based, considered a matter of justice by many and which make cultural sense in today's world. Subsequent generations in the Church (also impacted generally by the feminist movement in Western culture) in turn have had a positive experience of working collaboratively and now naturally employ these models. This has changed people's experience of church, of God and people, and it follows that the leadership repertoire of all, both male and female, is now inclusive of more than the dominant hierarchical model typically employed in the church. It only makes sense that emergent churches, made up of leaders impacted by this historical shift, and living at the church's power edge because of their age, would work collaboratively in ministry with a variety of people and perspectives, seeking to welcome and include all.

Liturgy reflects identity. It is the centerpiece of every sacramental Christian community. We are gathered through it, over time learning who we are by our interaction with, and embodiment of, word and sacrament. A parishioner who worships in a church in the round noted, 'We built a church in the round, and then the church in the round built us.' We shape what we do and what we do shapes us. We call this *lex orandi, lex credendi* in the Anglican tradition – 'the law of prayer is the law of belief'. We often interchange the terms and want to express 'we pray what we believe and we believe what we pray'. In Anglicanism, we would like to say that the process by which we establish liturgy engages this interchange to its fullest. We would want to claim that the process by which we study, collect and legislate liturgy allows all members to experiment with it to see if we discern its fruitfulness for ongoing use. Theoretically this gives as many people as possible a chance to engage in the *lex orandi, lex credendi* principle. Ultimately, however, authorization for us comes from those systemically empowered to make such decisions: clergy (and in the English system this gives bishops a particular role), committees, national synods and conventions. It usually does not include those on our power's edge, most notably those under the age of 40 who do not attend church.

In emergent churches, the process of *lex orandi, lex credendi* is more flat. It includes thoughtful, well-trained theologians and liturgists – both lay and ordained – and sometimes even those who may not yet have made a full commitment to the Christian life. We discovered in emergent churches that in preparing liturgy, groups study together, listen to one another's experience of Scripture, the tradition and the culture. They have a conversation. They take seriously their work of discerning and articulating the faith story of Christianity, and of creating space for participants to discover their own faith journey. Emergents would want to say that worship emerges out of the community, inspired by the Holy Spirit, mining the riches of the tradition of the church, but adhering to the rules of the institution secondarily. We experienced differing emphases in various communities, such as the personal faith journey, social justice, communication and exploration of the Christian faith. We observed creative use of both authorized texts and original texts appropriate to the season or occasion. The intent was always to create a liturgical environment in which people could fully participate in the worship, bring their own discernment and articulation of the faith, and experience a sense of belonging to the body of Christ. No matter the emphasis, we found the mode of liturgical creation consistently conversational: collaborative and inclusive of many voices, some not often heard in the institutional church.

This model of shared authority was also noted in who presided over worship. While in more sacramental settings it was nearly always a priest who celebrated the Eucharist, other roles were typically shared by any number of people, not usually authorized by the institutional church. Gospel readings were sung by musicians, prayers offered by the congregation, gestures of worship shared by the whole congregation, and the eucharistic elements passed by each person one to another. The traditional format for the delivery of a sermon in the institutional church is an offering of a prepared text by one, seminary-trained member of the clergy. In emergent churches we experienced sermons preached by laity, sermons responded to in conversation during a feedback time, or individuals creating their own reflections by participating in Open Space (see page 51). This is a clear shift in thinking about who is authorized to teach the faith, elevating the importance of personal experience and reflecting a desire to welcome into a public faith conversation the variety of perspectives found among those worshipping on any given occasion. There was, therefore, less expectation on the part of leaders of emergent churches that they would maintain authority over the beliefs of its members. In fact we heard little interest in doing so.

We came to use the term 'indigenous authenticity', as a descriptor of the way authority works in emergent communities and its impact on worship and communal life. All the congregations we visited were truly interested in, conscious of and connected to their ministry context. For some this context related to geographical community; for others it related more to non-geographical networks. The congregations invested in, belonged to, understood and expressed care for those in their communities, and there was consistent invitation to those seeking to be a partner in conversation about Christianity.

As the emerging church relates with the inherited church, inclusion of and collaboration between the two generates worship that is reflective of its participants, the doctrines and beliefs of the church and the ongoing faith conversation over time. In emergent communities liturgy given by the institution that has not been offered into the community for discussion and acceptance is not going to be utilized without question. The institutional church should not expect to hand down liturgical innovations to such communities, assuming acceptance. Nor should it seek to create just one process of liturgical review for all in order to encourage conformity. Authority does not work this way in emergent communities and it would be a violation of their soul, so to speak, to assume otherwise. This does not mean that emergent Christians will only use liturgy they create themselves, but it does mean that they are likely to have a local process by which they study and embrace texts that may become their own. In the description of Transmission (see page 34), for instance, one can identify a very different model of authority in the design and sharing of the liturgy.

Not only is the shared model of authority exercised within the church, it is also exercised outside of it. In emerging churches there is only a thin dividing line between those who belong and those who do not. Membership is much more porous than in the institutional church. The passion at the heart of emergent Christians is a deep desire to share the good news of God's love in Jesus Christ – above anything else. Promoting denominational membership is of little importance. Promoting an open system in every way possible in order to provide not just welcome but a community in which truly, all sorts and conditions of people may find Christ is of utmost importance. If they become an Anglican or an Episcopalian, that is great, but it is not the most important thing. 'Making' someone a Christian within a prescribed period of time is not a strategy for growth in these congregations. There is full acceptance in emergent churches that the society is completely secular and that the path to commitment may take years to develop, if at all. These too have a voice in the community.

Phyllis Tickle notes in *The Great Emergence* that even the reasons behind the way the institutional church makes decisions about what is authoritative are lost on the postmodern generation. What we experienced is what she sums up: that when asked where authority lies, emergent Christians will finally relent and say that it is found in the mix between Scripture and the community – not as handed down by the institution of the church, but rather as it is locally discerned by those in the body. She notes that one of the dynamics inherent in this current reformation-like period in which we find ourselves is that the source of authority is no longer assumed; that is, clearly identified as being from Scripture or tradition or experience, another named source or, as in Anglicanism, a combination of several. In Christianity, tradition, Scripture and revelation have been some of the primary 'authorizers' of liturgy, ritual and experience. The institution has been the gatekeeper of that reality. Tickle notes:

> The new Christianity of the Great Emergence must discover some authority base or delivery system and/or governing agency of its own. It must formulate – and soon – something other than Luther's *sola scriptura* which, although used so well by the Great Reformation originally, is now seen as hopelessly outmoded or insufficient.

For emergents, looking to an existing centralized authority to determine 'truth' on a particular matter is not why the church exists, nor does it make sense for an institution to use power and authority in a way that does not include conversation with the people involved. We experienced, and found that in many such communities this was understood, that people can gather in Christian community and not be in agreement about issues. Agreement is not a core value. In fact, several of these communities seek to include as much diversity as possible, wanting to live together and work through issues that may be personally divisive but where individual views – and personal authority to decide for oneself – are respected. This was yet another example of inclusion as an operating principle of authority, and certainly an illustration of how 'truth', understood by some more subjectively in the postmodern age, is authoritatively discerned locally by those engaged in the conversation and not by a single external source. For emergent Christians, this principle was a witness to the unifying presence of Christ, offering a positive and powerful voice of how to get along in a world fraught with so much division.

Tickle fleshes out the systemic reality of authority in emergent Christianity, concluding that 'crowd sourcing', itself integral to network theory, is how authority for emergents will work. She states:

The Church, capital C – is not really a 'thing' or entity so much as it is a network in exactly the same way that the Internet or the World Wide Web or, for that matter, gene regulatory and metabolic networks are not 'things' or entities. Like them, from the point of view of an emergent, the Church is a self-organizing system of relations, symmetrical or otherwise, between innumerable member-parts that themselves form subsets of relations within their smaller networks, etc., etc. in interlacing levels of complexity. The end result of this understanding of dynamic structure is the realization that no one of the member parts or connecting networks has the whole or entire 'truth' of anything, either as such and/or when independent of the others. Each is only a single working piece of what is evolving and is sustainable so long as the interconnectivity of the whole remains intact. No one of the member parts or their hubs, in other words, has the whole truth as a possession or as its domain. This conceptualization is not just a theory. Rather, it has a name: 'crowd sourcing'; and crowd sourcing differs from democracy far more substantially than one might at first suspect. It differs in that it employs total egalitarianism, a respect for worth of the *hoi polloi* that even pure democracy never had, and a complete indifference to capitalism as a virtue or to individualism as a godly circumstance.

This is a very different understanding of one of the functions of the institutional church in our respective contexts, historically involved in nation building and the stabilization of society, as determined by a dominant group, of which the institutional church was a part. How we understand authority, then, necessarily changes how we self-organize as a body and how we engage with the world around us.

There is a significant conversation for the institutional church to have with emergent communities. Each offers tremendous gifts to the other, but approaches the task of sharing the gospel differently, because we understand and employ authority differently. This divergence is a good place to begin the conversation. In our structure it makes sense that this will happen between bishops and emergent congregations, or more generally with those churches that want to explore what it takes to reach out to a postmodern society with the gospel of Jesus Christ. We found emergents open to this conversation, not at all resistant to the gifts of the institutional church. Indeed, they embrace the history and tradition of Anglican Christianity.

All the ordained emergent church leaders whom we met were clear on the importance of their link with their bishop. Their sense of accountability was often complex – to God, to their community, sometimes to a support or monitoring group, but always to the bishop, regarding themselves as a member of the college of priests in the diocese and grateful to the bishop for encouragement and permission to press some of the boundaries. This was the case even where the emergent communities themselves did not feel a strong sense of being linked into the wider Church; the priest/leader felt that link to be very important. There was often a stronger sense of relationship to the bishop as spiritual leader and pastor than to the diocese as an organization. The only emergent community where such a relationship was not in place would have welcomed such a relationship if it had been on offer. The bishop as pastor, encourager and permission giver is much needed. Where there is that relationship, the bishop can sometimes question and gently guide and restrain where things are going wrong or if the community is moving too far from the ethos of the diocese or the wider Church than is good for its own well-being and flourishing. We found no resistance to that kind of honest and creative relationship between bishops and emergent leaders.

The leaders we met on this pilgrimage were eager to speak with us as bishops about the challenges and successes of their ministry, and wanted very much to create a context for which the conversation they are having on the church's edge could be more inclusive of the institution itself. As throughout all of history, there is life on power's edge. Ironically, the institutional church increasingly finds itself off to the side of the way the dominant culture works. We have something profound, life-changing, rich and wondrous to share.

Worshipping communities 2: Transmission

New York – 17 February 2010

Transmission is a house 'church' meeting in the apartments of members of the church in the Manhattan district of New York. It came into existence in August 2006.

The initial leaders of Transmission were Bowie Snodgrass and Isaac Everett. Its leadership is now less easy to define and Bowie sees herself more as an adviser ('leader emeritus'), while Isaac continues in a more active role of liturgical leadership. In an interview with Bowie, we learned that both she and Isaac have Master of Divinity degrees. Bowie works full time as executive director for a multi-faith initiative called 'Faithhouse'. Bowie is heavily involved in St John the Divine Cathedral and has good networks into the emerging church world on both sides of the Atlantic. She previously worked at The Episcopal Church Center in New York.

Worship leadership is played down at Transmission in that roles rotate among the members, but Isaac is a key player. He is a theologically trained church musician in his late 20s, who has worked for Episcopal congregations, discerning ordination within the Lutheran Church.

Most of the members are in their late 20s and single. Isaac and Katie Everett are the only members married to one another. On the occasion we visited there were a couple of older members and a wonderful mixture of backgrounds, some with theological qualifications and a lot of knowledge of mainstream church, some with neither. The membership included Johannes, a young German who had recently arrived in New York, and a woman who was a recent convert from Judaism. On each occasion one person is host, another is the leader of the ritual (and its deviser) and a third is the cook.

We shared in Transmission on 17 February 2010, Ash Wednesday evening. On this occasion the gathering was at Isaac and Katie's apartment. People greeted one another as they arrived. We were made welcome. We sat on chairs in a circle in the quite small living room, in the corner of which was the kitchen area where the supper was cooking. On a table, almost as part of the circle, were two lighted candles, a large empty glass bowl and some flowers and herbs. There were no 'visuals' and the only music, other than our voices, was provided by two guitars, played by Isaac and Johannes. Katie led the 'ritual' and spoke confidently about Jesus, sacrifice and the cross.

We participated in the informal liturgy (described on page 96). This was an experience of ritual, but it is more difficult to know whether it could be termed worship. God was addressed, but only in the psalm and the songs. The words that came closest to prayer were the opening words, 'My soul thirsts for you'.

The liturgical elements present were singing, the use of Scripture, a talk that could be received as a homily, a time of reflection (when writing individually on papers that would be burned) and the ritual action. The Scripture included two readings, a responsorial psalm and a song that was also a biblical text (verses from Psalm 31). Liturgical elements that were missing included spoken prayer (whether penitence, praise, intercession or thanksgiving), greeting and peace-sharing, silence (other than when writing) and any acknowledgement of a world beyond the group. The Eucharist was not celebrated.

There was, of course, shared food and drink afterwards, but there was not an overt sense of this as a 'sacred meal' – there was not even a blessing of the meal. Though not a recognized liturgical element, perhaps it was surprising that there was no space for sharing and discussion within the time together. It was explained to us that whether these elements were included or not was up to the organizers of the ritual. Afterwards, as we shared in supper, there was a discussion, much of it about the mainstream church (perhaps influenced by the presence of two bishops!), but also about inclusivity in the church, the open table at Communion, and about independence and accountability in emerging churches such as Transmission.

In this post-service conversation we discovered that five of the evening's congregation had Master of Divinity degrees from Union Theological Seminary. There seemed a strong sense that this community was processing its relationship with the wider Church. Several of the members had connections with other mainline congregations (mostly Episcopal Church congregations), but also indicated that their exploration of being part of a larger body, such as a TEC (Episcopal) congregation, had not been met with much enthusiasm by the bishops. We wondered whether what appeared to be the insular identity of the group might have been challenged to be more outward focused – both towards God and towards the wider community – had they had a more clearly defined relationship with the diocese and its bishop.

4

The holiness of beauty

A Buddhist parable tells of a monk who was walking in the jungle one day. Suddenly a ferocious tiger began to chase him. He ran and ran, trying to outrun the tiger. Suddenly a beautiful, perfect strawberry appeared before him. He stopped running and took a bite out of it.

A picture paints a thousand words, they say. For most of us, something beautiful, verbally expressed or otherwise, can stimulate our imagination and move us to deep emotion and transformation, offering us a new perspective. A song, a story, a picture, God's creation, liturgy well done, can stop us in our tracks and make us suddenly aware of something larger than ourselves, our current struggles. We can be moved to another level of thinking and feeling, beyond the rational, having a spiritual experience, seeing with our hearts the unseen things of life: love, peace, joy, grace. In those moments when we are aware of more than meets the eye, there is no need to defend something as right or real. It resonates as holy, as true for our soul, in part because we are utterly convicted by its beauty.

Churches of all sorts have chased and been chased by the desire to grow, to be relevant in an age when Western churches seem so much less so in the general culture. We have pursued programmes, people, the latest trends and star-quality leaders seeking success. We have bought into the notion that if we import an idea, and do it just like someone else did, then we too will thrive at 'being church'.

Anglicans have occupied a unique place in the wider Church. We are distinct from Catholicism and Protestantism. We have a unique identity. One of Anglicanism's greatest treasures is the beauty of liturgy. Aesthetics matter to us. We understand that our souls are touched by the arts, and that our spiritual lives are deepened by beauty. Brian McLaren notes in *A Generous Orthodoxy* that this is what allows our tradition to hold together through so much diversity and tension.

Even if they disagree on what the liturgy means or requires doctri-
nally, they are charmed by its mysterious beauty and beautiful mystery.
That is often enough to keep them together long enough to share,
evaluate, and integrate varied understandings. In contrast to Christians
who argue about the fine points of doctrine but show little taste for
the beauty of truth, the Anglican way (as I have observed it) has been
to begin with beauty, to focus on beauty, and to stay with it, believing
that where beauty is, God is.

At our Anglican core is worship: beautiful liturgy meant to move the
soul, drawing us closer to God. Throughout our pilgrimage of emerging churches, we were moved many times by the sheer beauty of the
liturgy we experienced. Sometimes this occurred with innovative liturgies and sometimes with traditional ones we knew from memory. Emergent leaders we encountered were not chasing after the latest liturgical
trend in order to offer a beautiful and moving experience of church.
They drew from the well of Christian liturgical experience, Anglican
and otherwise, and engaged a conversation with their local context.
In this creative way liturgy emerges that is both holy and beautiful.

'Indigenous authenticity', as noted in Chapter 3, is how we have
described this process that does not impose liturgical expression but
allows it to be discerned in the community. While some who read
this book may be looking for a technique, a programme or some sort
of manual on how to be an emerging church, or even liturgically
innovative, we encourage such people to look more deeply at their
identity and to resist the more anxious response to change by copy-
ing something from somewhere else into their context. It is better to
take the time to know one's own tradition and community. There is
a lovely and simple chant by Amy McCreath that repeats the simple
line 'What we need is here', extracted from a poem by Wendel Berry.
As worshippers gather, one becomes aware of being in the presence
of a beautiful truth, and that all we need is already with us. Liturgical
innovations that we may need to make are already within our body. As
we discover them, we experience the holiness of beauty in our midst.

What is beautiful is generally understood to be in the eye of the
beholder. It is subjective from one person to another. The *Oxford
English Dictionary* gives as its first definition of beauty 'a combination
of qualities, such as shape, colour or form, that pleases the aesthetic
senses, especially the sight'. A secondary definition is 'a combination
of qualities that pleases the intellect or moral sense'. This second

definition broadens our understanding of beauty beyond the aesthetic. Our sense is that most emergents use it in this broader sense and we have used it in this way here. We encountered in some emergent worship an emphasis on aesthetic beauty and in others an emphasis on Anglican liturgical order that would be pleasing to the intellect. Both definitions of beauty were present, though not always at the same time. Sometimes the worship did not reflect a strong concern with aesthetics and might not be characterized as beautiful in the narrower sense. These offerings of worship, however, would probably be considered beautiful by emergents because they appealed to the intellect and moral sense, were authentic to that particular community, and focused on the spiritual journey. Paul, in his Letter to the Romans, encourages Christians to be 'transformed by the renewing of your minds' (12.2). Irenaeus of Lyons said, 'The glory of God is a human being fully alive.' Transformation of the individual itself is beautiful and holy, even if not accompanied by particular aesthetics.

Emerging leaders with whom we spoke and who have written on the subject affirm our observation that liturgy inspired and created locally was holy and beautiful precisely because it was local and authentic to those who offered it. This could be characterized as a value of emergent worship. All the services we attended were the result of careful planning, study and prayer that took into account Scripture, context of the worshipping community and wider culture, the gifts present in the community and the Anglican tradition. If there is nothing more beautiful, more appealing than a person who is fully themselves, so it is with Christian communities.

An illustration of this point is the contrast between St Paul's Episcopal Church in Seattle and Thad's in Los Angeles. While not an emerging church *per se*, St Paul's Seattle, a contemporary Anglo-Catholic congregation, exhibited worship, both holy and beautiful, with a completely traditional, authorized liturgy. There was an obvious 'posture' of confidence communicating that the congregation had locally discerned and embraced what was authentic worship for them. As a visitor to this congregation, it was easy to be swept up to fully participate in the liturgy because it was confident, well done and a genuine expression of the spiritual life of the body. It was simply *true*. This congregation reportedly was half its current size just five years ago. While offering satisfaction for the postmodern person's yearning for mystery, from the moment one read the bulletin – which stated, 'if you are unfamiliar with the ritual customs of The Episcopal Church, simply relax with the liturgy and let the rest of the congregation carry you in worship' – it was obvious that this community had a clear understanding of itself and was unafraid to express that identity with grace and confidence in its liturgy.

At the other end of the spectrum, Thad's (the Church of St Thaddaeus, but always called Thad's) in Los Angeles, a minimally sacramental community (and the least Anglican/Episcopal-looking of the churches we visited in America, although possessing qualities of an Anglican ethos), was equally authentic and indigenous in its worship. The Thad's community uses liturgy that many in our tradition would consider sparse. It was not beautiful worship in the traditional, aesthetic understanding. A worshipping group of about 150 meets each Sunday in a synagogue, with no Christian imagery anywhere in the space. Jimmy Bartz, Episcopal priest and pastor of this emergent congregation, a preaching station of the Diocese of Los Angeles, was seated on a stool with a music stand in front of him for a podium, wearing jeans and a shirt, with no clerical collar or other indication that he was a priest. A large band played original music off to the side of the small stage. Music and prayers used are often written by members of the congregation, some of whom work in the entertainment industry and have professional artistic talent. (At the time of writing, three of the 16 Thad's musicians were union professionals.) While the music (generally characterized as 'Americana') ranged from country to jazz, and the liturgy was barely noticeable as Anglican, it was wholly authentic to that community. Prayers and readings were done beautifully, people responded to the teaching with moving personal stories and reflections. Music was played by members of the congregation, with lyrics clearly emerging from the spiritual journey of the writers and composed with the context of Thad's in mind. People offered themselves in genuine confidence, and the shared journey of people finding God was apparent. They were unafraid to be themselves. Thad's, just as St Paul's, witnessed to the presence of God at work in their midst, and although the language of beauty might vary, invited worshippers into the beautiful presence of God in Christ, in order that their spiritual life could be transformed. Admittedly, while making a particular point with this illustration, St Paul's more clearly communicates Episcopal identity in its worship using traditional aesthetic beauty and also emoting a strong spiritual self in the community. One could argue that Thad's, representing a more evangelical style of Anglicanism, still extends the ethos of the Anglican tradition in its preaching and teaching, but not in its liturgy.

When a congregation engages with the spiritual journey together, discovering what it means to be the body of Christ in a particular place in time, necessarily the level of offering increases to something holy and beautiful. The quality of worship cannot help but rise. The process itself of creating liturgy that is expressive of the inner life of the congregation, as opposed to being a body that is trying to follow a programme, brings awareness of being on holy ground. So often, we adhere to the inherited texts of our tradition to the point of inhibiting the depth they were intended to offer. Opening one's prayer book to the customary page at the customary time and reciting what is written before us, without being fully present to the Spirit in our midst, has us going through the motions but not necessarily fully alive to the glory of God. It is probably not an overstatement to suggest that much of the liturgy we experienced on our travels was a deep expression of love for Jesus and for God's people. As we worshipped with very diverse bodies on our pilgrimage, we often had a sense that the liturgy offered was a response to the full giving of God's own self in Christ. Such indigenous authenticity in liturgy sometimes felt a bit like the story of Mary anointing Jesus' feet: an extravagant, vulnerable gift of great love. Of course, it is to be found also in the inherited church, though not always.

It is in the holiness of beauty that emergent Christians work out what is true, sorting through their beliefs as they greet Christian theology and doctrine in the liturgy. Phyllis Tickle suggests that 'orthonomy', a word that connotes 'correct harmoniousness' or beauty, means 'the employment of aesthetic or harmonic purity as a tool for discerning the truth – and therefore the intent and authority – of anything, be that thing either doctrine or practice'. She observes that this generation is confused by arguments around doctrine or historicity of Scripture. If it is beautiful, in some way, it is true. She states:

> An emergent, in observing heated debates or impassioned conversations about the factualness of the Virgin birth, for example, can truly be puzzled. For him or her, the whole 'problem' is just not 'there' in any distinguishable or real sense. For the emergent, as he or she will be quick to say, 'the Virgin Birth is so beautiful that it has to be true, whether it happened or not'.

Tim Keel notes in his book *Intuitive Leadership*:

> Just as Scriptures themselves contain more than the doctrinal raw
> material for systematic theologies but testify to the mysterious Deity
> beyond the words, so also are there traditions within Christian the-
> ology and practice that witness to knowledge that is more than mere
> comprehension. Traditional theology usually concerns itself with a
> certain approach to doctrine that focuses on the rational aspects of
> God. Alongside such traditional expressions of theology are mystical
> traditions that seek to apprehend and describe the non-rational, or
> perhaps supra-rational, aspects of God.

While the church claims a particular understanding of what is true
about God and has defended it through rational argument through
the ages, it is this experience of God in which emergents are interested and intrigued. God is to be experienced, more than rationally
understood. Hence, worship is not only aesthetically moving, but
designed for personal transformation in meeting Christ. As in traditional Anglicanism, beauty is purposeful, but not exclusively for the
communication of doctrine. Some in the institution would be ner-
vous about a sort of theological wandering and about where people
might or might not end up. Keeping the end in mind has always been
a focus of the church as it has shared the good news of Jesus Christ.
But it is the journey, precisely this engaging in spiritual wandering,
that is important to emergents.

Leaders we met embraced an understanding of the pastoral needs
of today, of the people they were serving. For so long, the church has
offered the sacraments as rhythm to the Christian, modern world,
Baptism and Marriage among them. In a secular society this rhythm
has given way to a myriad other pulses, some involving spirituality
(not religion), some not. There is no longer a societal pressure to be
baptized, or even married for that matter. Such pastoral needs once
common to society as a whole are now related to personal beliefs.
Yet, other common pastoral needs have emerged. Among these is the
need for the average person in the high-paced, high-tech Western
world to experience a sense of belonging. Loneliness, sense of purpose, a framework for how the world works and one's place in it,
and an understanding of God, are all pastoral needs that the church
needs to address now. We have answers to these questions and more.
The process by which one begins to discover one's life with God begins

with human beings, starting with one's own life experience and framework, and then moving into relationship with God. The discovery that one has a spiritual life is considered beautiful by emergents. Likewise, whether or not the doctrine of the incarnation is historically true (as one might surmise from Phyllis Tickle's comment on the virgin birth) is less relevant than the beautiful truth of God becoming human for the sake of love. The incarnation and its personal impact on the individual are no longer mere theological emphases, but the means by which this generation understands the progression of faith development. Such beauty provides a way into life with God.

By all accounts of those doing ministry with those who have no knowledge of God in Jesus, this process takes time and employs very different methods of bringing people to faith. It is an experience to be had, not a doctrine to be learned. Bev Robertson is the priest at St Nicholas' Church in Portsmouth, UK. On a Sunday morning it attracts a fairly conservative congregation of local people to its Eucharist. But Bev also has Ethos @ St Nick's to reach people alienated by traditional church and is seeking through it to serve a community well beyond her parish boundaries through something that begins in a very different place from the Sunday Eucharist. Bev noted that she uses texts and insights from other faiths – 'the beauty of other religions' – giving the Christian Scriptures special status because they speak of the significance of the loving relationship between God and humankind. She prefers not to use the word 'worship', since it is very unfamiliar in the common culture. Instead she prefers 'creating a sense of the sacred'.

Several congregations that we visited were intentional about ministering to people who had been hurt by the church, who needed an enlivening of their faith or an expansion of their image of God. One might suggest that in fact the purpose of these liturgies was to offer the worshipper the concept of the beauty of holiness and the holiness of beauty. Ethos @ St Nick's, on the night we visited, offered a particular way that was almost therapeutic, of reframing one's experience of God. Worship was oriented towards those who have been immersed in a theology of a judgemental and harsh God: imagery not generally considered aesthetically beautiful, or conducive to a graceful transformational experience. The theme of the evening was 'The Face of God'. The content of the liturgy, beautifully and sensitively done, offered participants a new way to experience the holy. Worshippers were invited to move through both positive and negative images of God, as well as that of a loving Jesus. The liturgy, using various writings to describe common negative experiences of God, was intended to help the worshipper get in touch with their own sense of who God was for them. Words were quoted from Gerald Priestland, for example: 'Sin kept cropping up in prayers, sermons and hymns. I gathered in some mysterious way it was my sin, my naughtiness, that had nailed that agonized figure to its wooden cross over the altar.' People were invited to choose images that reflected their sense of who God was for them, placing them collectively, like an offering. A beautiful meditation by Bev followed, expressing a loving and graceful God, whom we know in Jesus. Following the liturgy there was conversation where people could reflect their experience of it. This was holy and beautiful liturgy in every sense; aesthetically as well as in the offering of a transformational experience for one's spiritual journey.

While many existing churches would place much emphasis on the beauty of the space, and spend large sums of money to make it so, emergent congregations, usually not financially wealthy, seemed comparatively less concerned about this. This may be a matter of necessity, but in general they seemed more concerned about what went on inside the building rather than the building itself. For them, aesthetics are there to help a person arrive at what is really important, an incarnational encounter with the living God who gives us life in every way. Beautiful liturgical space is created with words, songs, movement and art. There is less reliance on the space to communicate. In fact, one might understand that the incarnational emphasis found in emergent Christians prioritizes the truth that God is found in people and the gifts they express, as opposed to structures or physical space.

On the other hand, the Church of St Gregory of Nyssa in San Francisco dwells in a very beautiful building. The community was founded by Don Schell and Rick Fabian, who in time became its co-rectors, in 1978, and thus predates the emerging church movement. Its liturgy, entirely integrated with its building, brings together the liturgy of The Episcopal Church, together with much Orthodox insight and practice, and with the inclusion also of materials from other faiths. The Jewish synagogue influence is particularly strong. St Gregory's has more than 300 'members', though its emphasis is not chiefly on membership, and on the Sunday we were present there were about 130 people sharing in the liturgy. St Gregory's purpose-built church, opened in 1995, has a clear theological messaging of inclusion and welcome in its placement of the altar, baptismal font and use of other liturgical items from a wide variety of Christian traditions. While not characterizing themselves as emerging, the beauty of their space and the well-orchestrated liturgy was a feast for all the senses and a powerful experience of the holy.

Some churches used visual images on screens, and in one service we attended an artist painted two paintings simultaneously throughout the otherwise quite traditional liturgy. This was not only fascinating, but helped create a meditative liturgical experience, where quite literally one could visually behold the holiness of beauty – and the beauty of holiness – in the making.

As Christians, what we inherit from ages past in tradition, liturgy and buildings are gifts to us. We should be good stewards of all that is handed from generation to generation. Whether we have the gift of good liturgical space or even high-tech audio-visual equipment, we now live in an age where we must communicate the faith more consciously, not depending solely on those things to do our faith-sharing for us. Individuals and congregations would be blessed by considering what the relationship between holiness and beauty is for them, and in what fresh ways that might be expressed for the next generation of people searching for God.

Words for worship 2: Meditations

Like a woman looking for treasure lost,
and a father waiting for his child,
like a shepherd seeking a straying sheep,
so is my longing for you.

Like a pearl hidden deep within,
and a treasure buried in a field,
like a seed planted in your soul,
so is my presence in you.

Like a girl woken from the depth of death,
and a woman restored to health,
like a tortured soul embraced by love,
so is my desire for you.

Like a kingdom laced with gold and pearls,
like a lover loving to the death,
like one who opened his arms in life,
so is my love for you.

Beverley Robertson

You say you know the face of God?
Then you must know the colour of love,
And the taste of music,
The smell of a sunset,
The sound of the moon.

Tell me the origin of your thoughts,
Number the beats of your heart,
Count the hairs on your head,
Show me where feeling lives.

No?
You or I can never see or know
The One who looks behind our eyes,
The One who breathes us in and out
And draws us on the page of time.

Let go of the God you carve with your mind.
Let go of all that safety and sameness.
Allow her to freely breathe
And let God be God in you.

Beverley Robertson

5

The reverberation of God's word

Transcendence (described on page 9) is a monthly alternative worship service in York Minster, one of the great English cathedrals. The service was developed by Visions, a fresh expressions community in York that is now nearly 20 years old. At its liturgy in February 2010, after the entry of the ministers, an opening song, prayers of penitence and a collect said together, we settled into the Liturgy of the Word. 'Settled' is probably not quite the word, for after the Sunday's set reading from the Old Testament, we were drawn into a short practice of the Alleluia response to the psalm, and then the entire community moved from the great vaulted round Chapter House of the Minster, where the liturgy was being celebrated, in an informal kind of procession, singing as we went, into the main body of the Minster, where the Gospel reading was chanted by the deacon. There followed a scripted homily, delivered by three ministers, speaking one after another, before we scattered around the Minster to one of five prayer stations.

The procession had something of the atmosphere of going on pilgrimage, the Book of the Gospels carried at our head, with the sense that we followed Christ. The movement and the walking together singing had the mood of approach to the holy place, in this case the holy place being not so much the arrival in the Minster nave as the encounter with Christ who, having gone before us, was waiting to welcome us, perhaps to transform us, for the Gospel reading on that day was Luke's account of the transfiguration.

The singing of the Gospel – slowly, confidently, prayerfully – was a moment of surprise. For years the church seems to have discouraged such a practice, plain speaking being much preferred and microphones making it unnecessary to chant in order for the voice to carry and be heard. But this was a beautiful moment, the sense of holy ground all the stronger, and communication at a deep level. A transforming moment.

Although both the processional movement and the singing of the Gospel were untypical, in other respects what was experienced at Transcendence was much in line with the practice of many of the emergent churches.

First of all, and most fundamentally, there was the reading of Scripture. There was no community that we visited where the Scriptures were not proclaimed. The word 'proclaimed' is used with care, because a straight reading of the text from an authorized and accurate translation was not always the case. At Thad's in Los Angeles a talented reader read the whole of Acts 22 in the version called *The Message* by Eugene Peterson, with its loose paraphrase and strong imagery – the Roman tribune causing the apostle Paul to be 'spread-eagled with thongs'! It was a powerful rendering.

Blesséd is a fresh expression that came into existence while Simon Rundle was Curate of Holy Spirit, Southsea, around 2004. It began as worship for young people, mainly 14 and 15 year olds, with sacramentally based worship, 'using the tools of Anglo-Catholicism'. Gradually a small team (now recognizable as the Blesséd community) came into existence, working with Simon to produce worship events. Simon speaks of Blesséd, now based at St Thomas' Gosport, as a 'non parochial community' and 'creating community out of gathering'. The worship happens about once a month and attendance can be anything between 20 and 70. On the eve of Mothering Sunday, which was a small gathering of just 20, the Gospel was proclaimed simply by a video clip of Mary at the foot of the cross with Jesus speaking the words, 'Behold, your mother, behold, your son.'

At Moot in London, whereas the first two readings were a straightforward delivery of the biblical passages, the Gospel reading (Luke 15.11b–32, the so-called parable of the prodigal son) was entrusted to a dramatic story-teller who brought the story alive, but sat light to the precise words of Scripture.

These were all dramatic and effective uses of the scriptural material, bringing out in the hearers a real attentiveness to the Bible message. Only in one place was the Scripture used in a way that might be thought unhelpful. Sanctus1 is one of the early fresh expressions. It is Anglican/Methodist sponsored, and meets in the centre of Manchester. It describes itself as: 'a Christian community exploring spirituality in contemporary culture. Sanctus1 seeks to push at the boundaries, exploring God and spirituality within the city, in contemporary film and art, and within each other.' At the midweek gathering one evening in January, with a dozen young people present and where the theme of the evening explored the place of rules in the Christian life, the only passage of Scripture read was part of Leviticus 13, relating to leprosy, mildew and clothes. The point of reading this obscure passage appeared to be to draw out the foolishness of rules. But this was untypical and, to be fair, it may have been untypical of Sanctus1.

Second, the Transcendence experience was also typical of many emergent churches in having a serious engagement with Scripture in terms of how much of it we heard. In the majority of them there were two or three readings and in six of them there were psalms.

Third, there was a frequent use of the lectionary, keeping in step with the rest of the church. One fresh expressions leader commented, 'When you see the need to do something other than preach about the cross every week, you come to value the Christian year and go to the lectionary.' Consistently we experienced emergent churches engaging the Scriptures as handed on by the Anglican tradition; not picking and choosing readings as they desired, but engaging the full salvation story as it was handed on to the church today.

The Revised Common Lectionary, in use in both Britain and America, has no pre-determined themes. Those who use the lectionary are invited to explore the set Scriptures to see what themes emerge for them. We often saw very effective use of themes, aside from the church season being celebrated. Sometimes the themes expanded on the season very purposefully. We visited several churches in Lent. For The Crossing in Boston (see page 55), on the second day of Lent, the evening's theme was 'Wilderness', taken from the Gospel account of Jesus being tempted by Satan in the wilderness. At the Church of the Apostles (see page 105), the Lenten theme was 'Faithful Wandering', reflecting on the truth that while one may have a sense of being lost, God is leading one home. Thad's Lenten theme was 'Your baggage – God's got it.'

Although it was only at Transcendence that we were all invited to follow the Book of the Gospels into another space, this was not the only community in which the reading of the Gospel was a particularly engaging experience. At The Crossing, under the title 'The Good News', we heard Luke 4.1–13 (Jesus in the wilderness for 40 days). It was preceded by a gong and the singing of a beautiful chant, 'Open my heart'. The Gospel was sung by a female vocalist in an expressive lilting, haunting tone, reminiscent of the traditional chant yet with a more contemporary feel to it. At the end of the singing of the Gospel the gong and the chant were used again.

At St Gregory of Nyssa in San Francisco, on the First Sunday of Lent, after the initial gathering rite leading into prayer, a lay person read the First Reading, from Deuteronomy, at the end of which the cantor rang the pot bells and silence was kept for two minutes; after that the tingsha (hand cymbals) were sounded. We stood to sing a hymn and a deacon brought the reader, a lay person, to the lectern. A deacon announced the Gospel (Luke's account of the temptations), but the lay person read it, and afterwards the deacon walked towards the presider's chair, carrying the book and singing 'The Gospel of the Lord' as he went. The cantor rang the pot bells, silence was kept for two minutes and then the tingsha were sounded.

After the sermon and some responses from members of the congregation, we were invited to sing an Alleluia (St Gregory's retains Alleluias in Lent, following eastern custom), during which, said the presider, 'we will carry the Gospel Book around for you to greet with a touch, a kiss or a bow. If you can't reach the Book, please put your hand on the shoulder of someone who can.' As they moved among us the vested party smiled, made eye contact, touched people while singing and moving, but without making conversation.

At St Paul's Seattle, on the Second Sunday of Lent, a lay person read the Genesis reading set for the day with sensitivity. We noted how the three ministers behind the altar focused their eyes, quite intently, on the reader throughout the readings. The whole congregation sang verses of Psalm 27 to a very simple chant, unaccompanied and slowly. The same lay person read the Philippians reading with equal sensitivity, in fact with great beauty, and there followed what the service sheet described as a time of 'silence and stillness' – and it was indeed that, real stillness with a community silently engaged with the Scriptures for more than a minute. Everyone then stood to sing the Sequence Hymn, a cantor sang the Tract (being Lent there were no Alleluias, following Western custom), the Gospel was announced, the Book of the Gospels censed and the Gospel, from Luke 13, read from near the front of the nave, all turning towards it.

It is important to understand that part of the function of the Open Space element of worship in many emerging churches is to explore the Scripture readings. We experienced Open Space built into the worship at Ethos @ St Nick's in Portsmouth, Transcendence, The Crossing, the Church of the Apostles in Seattle and Moot. It is clearly an established part of emergent church worship. Open Space is the preferred term in the United States. In the UK this stage in the worship is more often called Stations. Both terms make sense. Open Space is what is being provided, an opportunity for people to have space to think, reflect, pray or simply to be. Open Space is created by a series of 'stations' around the building. In some places they are very specifically for prayer. At Transcendence they were described as 'prayer stations'. In some communities they are space to take forward what has been heard in a homily or in the dialogue or discussion that may have followed that, and we return to the use of Open Space for this purpose in the following chapter. Sometimes they are simply for exploring the readings.

At the Church of the Apostles (COTA), on the Second Sunday of Lent, after the three lectionary readings and the singing of Psalm 27, Open Space was introduced with a note indicating that normally there is at this point a sermon, but in Lent we would move straight from the readings to Open Space. 'Your faithful wandering through the various prayer stations is a reverberation of God's word for you and within you this Lent. This is your time with God.'

Three stations engaged directly with the three readings. Many churches might have shied away from the first reading (Genesis 15.1–12, 17–18). It is a particularly difficult and obscure passage where Abraham is asked by God to 'bring me a heifer three years old, a female goat three years old, a ram three years old, a turtledove, and a young pigeon', which Abraham has to cut in two. It is the moment of the making of a covenant, but it is not easy to understand. At COTA one of the stations was an 'Old Testament Theology Wall'. You stood at the wall, and fixed to the wall was this text and another from Deuteronomy, together with an extract from a scholarly commentary. This was serious Bible study. A second station was described as a 'Travel Journal'. Here we sat or knelt on the floor with the text of the Philippians reading and were invited to write down our thoughts. A third station featured candles and sand, with an invitation to explore the Gospel reading while focusing on the words 'I long to gather you up like a hen gathers her brood'. For 15 minutes or so the congregation of about 80 moved around the stations (there were five altogether, the other two less directly related to the readings), or stayed with just one of them, or sat in the body of the meeting space in quiet reflection.

It is significant that the liturgy was taken seriously and went with the church's observance of Lent, even to the extent of loyalty to the lectionary on a day when the Old Testament reading was so challenging. In theory, postmodern people and contemporary American Christianity come to church with a 'mall' mentality, as Bryan Spinks has argued in his book *The Worship Mall*, in that they pick and choose what they do and don't want, and leave the rest. While the use of the lectionary reflects a balanced and traditional offering of Scripture, people's response is left up to them. There is little critique about its orthodoxy or orthopraxy, simply an individual movement towards what one is drawn to, without judgement of one's self or one another. This is most apparent in the Open Space, where one can choose which Scripture one might want to engage with more deeply – or not. So there is no need to exclude an obscure passage, for people will have no problem in ignoring it if it does not come alive for them. It is safe to say that there was a sense of security and belonging among the worshippers at COTA – and at other emerging services we attended. The emergent church atmosphere consistently conveys that one belongs, no matter who you are or where you are on your journey. But what was very certain was that however much there was a culture of picking and choosing, Scripture was taken very seriously. Here, as elsewhere, there was real devotion to it.

Seriousness about the Scriptures was not restricted to those who stayed with the lectionary. At Thad's in Los Angeles, which has a less liturgical flavour, the decision not to stay with the lectionary had been a conscious one. But this community has spent 62 weeks reading and studying 2 Corinthians, 90 weeks on Luke's Gospel, and now, following eight weeks on the Hebrew Scriptures, had been many weeks on Acts.

We were surprised at first at the frequent use of psalmody, given that the saying and singing of psalms in many mainstream churches has declined. Isaac Everett, co-leader of Transmission in New York, has recently published a whole book of them, *Emergent Psalter*, which uses the text of the Book of Common Prayer of The Episcopal Church with only small changes and with musical settings in a variety of styles. At Transmission we sang Psalm 63 with a gentle and memorable refrain, 'My soul thirsts for you, my body yearns for you', at the beginning of the liturgy, and later a song that was also a version of verses from Psalm 31. At the Church of the Apostles, the whole community read Psalm 27 after the lectionary readings and sung between the spoken verses an extended antiphon:

Since I am sick,
Since I am in need,
Since I have no healing within me,
You are my help and my redeemer.

Safe Space in Telford, a new town in the English West Midlands, came into existence in 2006. It sees itself as an 'emerging/missional community'. It says of itself, 'Our "DNA" consists of three elements in relationship: community, pilgrimage and mission.' It gathers on Thursday evenings at the home of its leader, Mark Berry, on the edge of Telford for what it calls 'The Table'. The core community numbers about ten. In the worship in which we shared, Psalm 130 was read as the only passage of Scripture. At Ethos @ St Nick's Psalm 139 was used in a similar way.

It seemed to us that the use of the psalms met a pastoral need. The psalms speak with wonderful honesty of the variety of emotions that human beings experience, including confusion, desolation and sickness. So many people coming into the emerging churches are searching for security, healing and love in a world where these are in short supply and often where their lives have been damaged. The liturgy in general can be used as therapy. The psalms particularly meet these personal longings.

To complete the picture, it needs to be said that behind a full use of Scripture and, in many cases, a respect for the lectionary lies a real commitment in the emergent churches to the Christian year. Even where the lectionary is not followed, there is a strong reliance on the particular character of the seasons. In every single church we visited during Lent the focus was on the season and its themes, engaging with temptation, penitence and the approach of Holy Week and Easter. The biblical stories associated with the season were implicit even when they were not read. At Thad's, during the 'dialogue' after the sermon, a young man talked about never having been before in a church where Lent was kept and that this experience of it had been transformational for him, 'even though I really don't want this now!' For some in emergent churches, mainly those with a background in evangelical churches, the Christian year has been a welcome discovery. Some emergent church leaders regard it as one of the distinctive elements in their worship.

What is evident here, despite a huge variety of approach, is a deep and reverent commitment to the Bible, serious study of it, and frequent use of it, much of the time in step with the rest of the church. How it is expounded and understood and what authority is given to it is, of course, the next question and it is to questions of doctrine and truth that we turn in the next chapter.

Worshipping communities 3: The Crossing

Boston – 18 February 2010

The Crossing is an emergent church community that meets each Thursday evening at St Paul's Cathedral in Boston, USA. It was started by the Reverend Stephanie Spellers ('Rev Steph') who was ordained to serve in the cathedral in 2005. Soon after her arrival she was asked to begin a worship service for a missing age group, so she gathered around her a small number of people to prepare over some months for what emerged in 2006 as The Crossing.

The cathedral is an early nineteenth-century 'Georgian' building, over-filled with painted pews and with little flexible space. Nevertheless The Crossing has chosen to meet there, moving the altar and other furnishings in the chancel/sanctuary area to create a worship space that will comfortably fit about 50 people, with the use of the nave for some of the stations that often form part of the worship. Like most churches of its period, it does not have a natural ambience of mystery and worship. It comes out of the architecture of the Age of Reason and so one has to work particularly hard to create holy ground. The Crossing has succeeded.

We visited on the second day of Lent. The community has 50–60 members, which is larger than most genuine emergent churches, and Stephanie believes that it can continue to grow. Of the 50 or so present when we visited, 80 per cent or more were young people in their 20s or 30s, but some older people (not just us!) were entirely welcomed and incorporated. The congregation was largely white and included gay and lesbian people, of which The Crossing is inclusive. The community is also clear in saying that people representing a wide variety of social and political views attend The Crossing, where broad tolerance of difference is a strong value. Rev Steph is African American and employs a natural and authentic leadership style, giving permission for others to be themselves as full participants in whatever capacity they may be called to serve. It felt as though no matter who people were or what their experience was, there was a safe and deep sense of being spiritually at home in the congregation.

For most of the members, The Crossing is their sole church membership. Most have a Christian background, but had become disillusioned with church as they were experiencing it. There have

55

been several who have come through The Crossing to Confirmation, but none yet to Baptism. The group comprises a significant portion of the cathedral's life; the usual Sunday eucharistic community is only about 70. Because of its growth The Crossing is having to explore afresh the physical setting of its worship. It is fast outgrowing the restricted area of the cathedral chancel.

The Crossing is a eucharistic community. In the early days, its leaders reached the conclusion that this was the most satisfying form of worship into which to welcome people. It is in many ways a trad-itional liturgical community in terms of form, investing ancient and conventional practices with new vitality (or 'groove').

On the night we visited, it appeared customary that people were welcomed upon arrival with a greeting that set them at ease and contributed to a relaxed atmosphere. People stood around and talked in groups or went straight to the worship space. Gradually the com-munity gathered. Most sat on chairs on either side of the chancel, some on cushions between the chairs on the floor. Stephanie and Justin (the evening's lay preacher) sat on high stools in front of the altar. Music was live and of high quality, provided by three musicians with keyboard, synthesizer, single drum and vocalist. A singing bowl was used as a gong to move the liturgy on at key moments to the next stage. The lighting was low. There was a folded A4 service sheet. There was no projection screen for words or images.

This service felt like engaged spiritual worship, directed to God, focusing on Jesus. It also felt like liturgy, conventional in its euchar-istic shape, fresh and energized in its celebration.

Apparent throughout worship was the careful intention with which every detail had been planned and thought through, not for the purposes of control, but for participatory inclusion of a variety of people and the experiences they bring with them to worship at any given service. Participants appeared at ease, centred and prayerful from the start. The participation of all was ensured because of the design; and also because of the communication through word and gesture both of the leaders and of those already familiar with the liturgy.

There was a sense of beauty, not in the building (for in fact it was not very beautiful!), but in the worship itself, and in its authenticity. While well prepared, there was no sense of performance, but rather a genuine offering emerging – that indeed was lovely because it came out of the spirit of the group as it was gathered that night. The care with which every detail was handled, the preparation of the leader's words, patens and chalices, the gifts of art, song and self that were given forth by the congregation, all reflected an offering of the natural or real beauty of God's creation meeting up with the beauty of God's own self. This seemed a positive reflection of how emerging churches who seek to allow authentic spirituality and religious expression (that is a corporate response to God in our lives) can be fed by the tradition of Anglicanism, a tradition which values beauty in worship because it reflects something of God and draws out the best offering in ourselves.

6

Appropriating the church's faith

St Mark's Episcopal Cathedral in Seattle is not an emergent church and its liturgy is not 'alternative'. Its Sunday Eucharist is conventional and so, in a sense, is its late-night Compline, held each Sunday. What makes it quite extraordinary is the fact that every Sunday evening, just before 9.30 p.m., 500 or 600 people, most of them in their 20s, make their way up the hill to the cathedral. It has happened every week for more than 50 years. They enter the cathedral quietly. They find a place to sit or to lie down.

We were there on 28 February 2010. The pews were almost full, but so was the floor space around the altar and there were people in every corner. Some had brought rugs and cushions on which to lie. Some were couples, with arms around one another or holding hands. There was no sense of any space being off-limits. The cathedral had dimmed lighting. Before the service there was almost complete silence.

The men of the cathedral choir entered, robed in cassocks and surplices, and moved to the back, so that during the worship they were heard, but not seen by most of the 'congregation'. At 9.30 p.m. they sang the ancient monastic office of Night Prayer (Compline), with the traditional words and the traditional plainsong chants. The congregation listened, remaining entirely silent and still. It is difficult to describe how powerful this silent, still, shared experience was. The only additions to Compline or deviations from it were the use of the appointed psalm of the day instead of one of the traditional Compline psalms, the reading of the Gospel of the day, and a long polyphonic Latin anthem just before the final words of Compline.

There was one extraordinary moment. As the choir began to say the Apostles' Creed, the entire congregation stood up, those who had been lying as well as those sitting, and turned to the east while the Creed was recited. Fewer church communities than in the past follow this custom of facing east for the Creed, but it originates in the idea of turning to the east to face the rising sun, symbolic of the Risen Christ, at the profession of faith in Baptism. Few of those who stood and faced east in St Mark's Cathedral will have known about the origins of this ritual act, but we experienced it as at least an identification with the church and her teaching even if not, in every case, or perhaps the majority of cases, a profession of personal faith. Nobody joined in orally; this was listening worship.

Although this was a remarkable occasion, all the more so for the fact that it happens every week, it was not difficult to understand why people came. All these elements contributed. There was the experience of solidarity, being part of a large gathering and a very special, rather understated kind of community. There was the impact of the absolute stillness. There was the freedom to adopt any posture that was helpful. There was the sheer beauty of the ancient, timeless music well sung in the darkened building. There was the lack of any demand to speak; only to listen or simply to let the liturgy flow over you and through you.

This service was noted in a Seattle newspaper as being one of the top ten date spots for that city – perhaps a place of spiritual nurture for relationships. Along with couples attending worship, there were individuals present who were maintaining yoga poses for long periods of time, journalling, and, as was the case for everyone attending, deeply prayerful and attentive to contemplation, meditation and the inner life. As one young woman apparently told the Bishop of Olympia when asked why she faithfully attended this service, 'I don't go in for that church shit, but I need something more, and this is my something more.'

It was intriguing and a reality-check to watch this crowd come together for such a brief, silent worship opportunity, and yet recognize some deep bond in that place. The worship is of the 'performance' variety and one might think that little community-building or commitment is happening. The response, though, is one of active silence which cannot be assessed by words spoken or some physical response, and which clearly comes from needs being met. The cathedral pamphlet on the Compline service, notes:

> the interest in and attraction to the Compline service exists within the context of a society in general and a Christian Church in particular that have become increasingly secularized. Throughout the years, however, the singing of Compline has attempted to speak of other values. With its ministry directed toward spiritual values that nurture the soul,

it is engaged in a radical activity, to act contrary to the icons of contemporary society – money, power, material comfort. These values cannot sustain or nourish the soul.

It may seem difficult to discern the level of commitment in the community, but in fact quite a few people who have come forward for ordination in the Diocese of Olympia have had their first exposure to The Episcopal Church at this service. It is a witness to the Church that we do not always need to know, understand or measure the outcome of our offering, and that we should faithfully initiate worship ministries not based on what we consider to be an outcome favourable to the Church, but on what God is doing – aloud and silently, seen and unseen, now and in the future. Likewise, Compline at St Mark's speaks to a reality of many young people – they are interested in spirituality, but not necessarily religion. This may be a stage of life, but the institution would be wise to hear that Generation X and beyond will be far less interested, even as they age, in the maintenance of an institution than previous generations. In other words, the institution exists for the feeding of the soul – and for little else.

The story of Compline in St Mark's Cathedral could be told in several of the chapters of this book, for it speaks into several of the issues that we are exploring. But we have placed it here because of that quite extraordinary moment where more than 500 young people, hearing the words 'I believe in God', got up, faced east and stood in reverent stillness while the Creed was recited, then sat or lay down again. It was the tenth visit of the tour. It was the first time we heard the Creed (other than the confident singing of it earlier that day in St Paul's Seattle) and we were to hear it only once more. And we heard it, in this context, as something to which people listened respectfully, rather than as something they spoke for themselves.

It might be helpful to move for a moment to London and to the gathering on 14 March at St Mary Woolnoth Church of the new monastic community Moot (described on page 130). This was the one community where everyone was invited to share in the saying of the Creed. The service was the Eucharist and after the homily and stations, when we came back together, under the title of 'Affirmation of Faith' we said the Apostles' Creed, with a marginally amended text, repeating it clause by clause after a leader, with a drum accompaniment, as a kind of rap, the service sheet printing the text with the emphasized words in bold to help with the rhythm. This was a different approach to credal orthodoxy. Whereas most emergent churches simply do not use the creeds, Moot used the Apostles' Creed with some changes: 'I believe in God our Parent . . . God will come to judge the living and the dead . . . I believe in the resurrection of our earthly bodies.'

In conversation with Moot's priest-missioner, Ian Mobsby, we talked about the attitudes of those drawn to Moot that had led to the changes of words in the liturgy, with some implication for theology and orthodoxy. Ian had met a huge resistance to the use of 'Father' because of the experience of some of the community. Real difficulty emerged in the conversation that was stimulated by the traditional prayers of the church, such as the Lord's Prayer and the Creed, which contextually were seen to be overly male. There was also a desire to balance 'redemptive' with 'incarnational' theological language. Unchurched people found much Church of England traditional liturgy 'overly redemptive' in its language. Much of it he saw as a strong reaction against a penal substitution doctrine of atonement. It has taken six years to be able to introduce a version of the Creed and still not everybody is happy about it. Similarly it has taken till now to be able to explore the concept of sin and to help people see it as something different from the church imposing narrow guilt-inducing behavioural norms. To that extent Moot is a changing and developing community, working through these things together and gradually coming to a new and deeper understanding of the church's belief. Ian believes that he has brought the community to a point where tradition is understood as a positive thing, but it has been hard and not everybody, of course, is in the same place. Thus, although they have spoken of the Creed as 'about how we live', some people are still reluctant to say it.

Alongside listening to the Creed in St Mark's Cathedral and saying a version of it at Moot, we need to place the practice of the other emergent churches. At Home in Oxford and The Crossing in Boston, which followed a conventional eucharistic shape and used the lectionary, the teaching time led into meditation and prayer (at The Crossing, in Open Space stations), not into a creed. Nor was there a creed at St Gregory of Nyssa or the Church of the Apostles. Even Transcendence, which follows the Church of England's *Common Worship* order and uses only authorized texts, omitted the Creed, allowing the stations to take its place.

What emerges here is not, in general, a suspicion of theological orthodoxy, but simply of credal statements and the requirement to sign up to a particular definition of faith that may feel or actually be disingenuous. At Moot we found real debate about theological language, both in relation to God and in relation to our human nature, with some finding the concept of sin difficult to handle. And in some of the other communities we encountered a need, more than in most churches, to free God of gender, to speak sometimes of God as Mother and to find fresh ways of speaking about the persons of the Trinity. But the overwhelming message was one of confidence in the Scriptures and of theological orthodoxy.

This was certainly the case in the exploration of the Scriptures through sermons and homilies. Sometimes they were called by another name, but clear Christian teaching there certainly was.

Home is a fresh expression in Oxford, formed seven years ago, which we visited on Sunday 31 January. It meets at present each Sunday at 5 p.m. in St Mary and St John's Church, normally in the main Victorian Gothic church, but in deep midwinter in a fairly small enclosed chapel. On the day that we went there were fewer present than usual, 12 adults and four children. Part of the Eucharist was described as 'Listening for the Word of God – Listening to your Life'; after the lectionary reading the leader, Matt Rees, led what was called 'Discussion and Meditation'. He used an outline he had prepared and printed out, moving through four stages, each posing some questions, each inviting some contributions by others. It was a gentle, quite tentative exploratory time. It felt more like meditation with the occasional prompt than discussion, though Matt said it was not always like that.

At Transcendence, after the singing of the Gospel of the transfiguration, there was a scripted homily, the deacon speaking about Moses, the subdeacon about Elijah and the president about Jesus, each for about three minutes, with the projection of a changing icon of the transfiguration on the screen. It was followed by an invitation spoken with strong conviction – 'Let us pray' – that sent people scattering to the prayer stations around York Minster.

At Transmission on Ash Wednesday, meeting in the home of Isaac and Katie Everett, after three readings (two of them biblical) Katie gave a carefully thought-through talk about the Lent ritual we were about to follow (involving the use of ash, see page 96), reminding us that sacrifice is not always sacrifice for sin, but may be an offering of joy. Within this disarmingly simple talk was a sophisticated exploration of the theories of atonement.

The fact that Katie was leading the worship is very significant. We talked about it next day with Bowie Snodgrass, the co-founder of Transmission. Bowie spoke of people in their late 20s needing to 'reconstitute themselves'. It was as if 'they were shipwrecked out at sea and needed to put out their oar and row to solid shore'. We discussed the order of 'belong, behave, believe' versus 'believe, behave, belong', understanding that in the reconstituting, the rowing so to speak, it will be the case that postmodern people identify more strongly with the first configuration and the church historically expects the second. This is a major cognitive dissonance between the church and the current society, in that postmoderns inherently question everything, assumptive of their choices in life, are varied in their regard for institutions, from ambivalence to distrust but rarely blindly trusting, and are not, as a rule, going to believe without a process of exploration, understanding and commitment. Katie is on a spiritual journey that she says is unlikely to lead to Baptism. She told us that she chooses not to affiliate with any specific religious group and, if forced to choose a label, would probably call herself an atheist. She is drawn to Transmission because it is a welcoming environment in which one may explore spirituality and philosophy regardless of background or religious affiliation. She led the ritual from this spiritual place, theologically very accurate in her homily on the various understandings of atonement.

At St Gregory of Nyssa, after the Gospel reading the presider preached the sermon, seated at the chair with the Gospel Book propped up on his knees, at the end of which the cantor rang the pot bells, silence was kept for one minute and then the tingsha were sounded. The presider invited us to complete the sermon together. Three people in turn spoke briefly relating the sermon to their own experience. It was apparent that the presider was controlling how long the conversation would continue and was therefore able to offer some boundaries to what was being communicated.

At Thad's Jimmy Bartz preached a sermon of 25 minutes, seated on the presidential stool, very much a 'teaching chair'. It was strong biblical preaching around their Lenten theme of 'Your baggage – God's got it'. What followed was called 'Dialogue', though it was not so much dialogue as a series of independent and in some cases moving testimonies arising from the sermon, this section of the service lasting about 20 minutes.

As we noted in the previous chapter, the natural follow-on to the homily and the discussion that follows it in some communities is Open Space, a series of stations around the church or meeting place that people choose to explore. As has been said already, some of them are very directly shaped to reflect on the day's readings. Some lead people straight into prayer. At Transcendence and at COTA one was for the laying on of hands and anointing for healing. Some are overtly intercessory. But fundamentally they are what the title suggests: opportunities to explore faith and spirituality, sometimes by reading the material provided, sometimes by symbolic action, sometimes by art work, sometimes by sitting and thinking or gazing, always individually, privately, and almost always gently leading you into prayer. Most stations are silent spaces, though some have one or two for personal ministry or other conversation. It is important to understand that these stations have usually been created not by a worship leader but by other members of the community, who have met in advance of the liturgical occasion to wrestle with the theme of the readings and then to devise the stations. The point was made to us that having a share in this devising, preparing stage was understood as key participation more than having an upfront role during the worship itself. Eliacín Rosario, who is Catalyst for the Mustard Seed Community and whom we met at COTA, argues that 'the new epistemology requires a new pedagogy'. In other words a new way of teaching faith can be seen in many emergent churches in a cycle that moves from communal preparation of theological themes, through verbal encouragement and homily, followed by discussion into open space where people work to make what they can of what they have heard on their own.

Karen Ward of COTA spoke of the concept of 'little altars' – the side chapels of cathedrals and great churches, smaller spaces, each unique, filled with statues, paintings, candles, stained glass and text, where people might worship and pray. The Second Vatican Council swept these aside, so that in Roman Catholic churches they often stand abandoned and unadorned. Anglicans have, on the whole, kept them in place and continued to use and beautify them, but something of the spirit of that abandonment has nevertheless affected Anglicans as well. The liturgy is focused on one altar, one celebration, one intention, thoroughly corporate, in part a reaction against the individualism of the private mass. The Open Space concept in emergent churches is a kind of return to the little altars. Around the building are the stations, like little chapels, and you choose which one(s) to visit and there you engage in a personal and privatized way, though you do, at least if the worship is eucharistic, return to the 'high altar' and the shared celebration. This may be said to mark a return to complexity, which we discuss in Chapter 9.

The absence of creeds should not be taken to mean an avoidance of the recitation of the story of salvation in Jesus Christ. It was significant how many of the communities visited used a full and rich Eucharistic Prayer, in some cases from an authorized rite, more often improvised, but theologically rich and liturgically conventional. Indeed at both The Crossing and COTA we experienced extemporary Eucharistic Prayers, beautiful in their language and confident in their theology, celebrated in a way that drew us deeper into the mystery of Christ's death and resurrection.

So what emerges is a picture of orthodox Christian communities, proclaiming the historic faith of the church, not dumbing it down, sharing it with energy and commitment, engaging with theology creatively, inviting participation, recognizing that people are at different places on a journey, trying to provide for each person where they are, reluctant to move beyond proclamation into requiring assent, which is how a communal recitation of a creed would be understood. The understanding that one is free to choose one's spiritual path and not required to 'buy in' to a particular faith expression is a quality of postmodern thinking and emergent worship. One does not have to subscribe to a particular understanding of God in order to belong to any one of these communities.

In the end, the communities we encountered are not motivated to defend the Christian faith or denominational loyalty, but instead seek to create environments in which one's faith, one's truth, may be discovered. It may appear that for them faith and truth are more subjective than in the institutional church, where it is expected that certain beliefs will be articulated, even if not held. Emergent churches we visited were clear about the Christian message they offered, but never manipulated an outcome. Stephanie Spellers, priest at The Crossing, notes, 'We say, "Here is what the Christian faith is. What do you think?"' In addition to a worship environment that helps people discover truth for themselves, the Church of the Apostles hosts regularly a Theology Pub, in which a variety of topics are presented and discussed. The night we visited COTA, Dietrich Bonhoeffer was 'on tap'.

It may appear that emergent churches encourage a very subjective faith experience. But at the heart of coming to faith is the question, 'What is truth?' In the Gospel according to John, Pilate asks this of Jesus, who prompts the question by saying, 'Everyone who belongs to the truth listens to my voice' (18.37b). John's Gospel would want the reader to conclude that the Truth is 'who' and not 'what'. Pilate asks a question to which most human beings seek an answer. Are there certain things in the universe that are real, that are true? Is there something, or a way of seeing the world, that simply is? This is distinct from claiming something as true for one's own life, one's own perception of reality.

Peter Rollins, in *How (Not) to Speak of God*, distinguishes between Truth with a capital 'T' and truth with a small 't' to delineate the difference. With this understanding, we can grasp that there is the Truth of Christianity as expressed in the doctrines and creeds of our faith, and there is one's experience of it. While the first is offered, it is personal engagement with what is True, what is Real, that nourishes the soul. Belonging, listening to the voice of Jesus, who says of himself that he is the Truth, produces faith, what is true for ourselves. Rollins notes, 'Truth is thus understood as a soteriological event'. Soteriology refers to salvation, implying cure, remedy or healing. He states further:

> the Judeo-Christian view of truth is concerned with having a relationship with the Real (God) that results in us transforming reality. The emphasis is thus not on description but on transformation. This perspective completely short-circuits the long-redundant debate as to whether truth is subjective or objective, for here Truth is the ungraspable Real (objective) that transforms the individual (subjective).

We experienced emergent leaders as uninterested in people repeating words of faith separate from their experience of transformation. They are committed to creating an environment for people to discover whatever is true for themselves, as they experience Truth. The clergy we met were seminary trained and very capable Christian leaders. They created liturgy and shared the Truth as Christianity in our context understands it. They are skilled in the discussion and development of theology, but their passion is in sharing the incarnational reality of Jesus as God, helping others also be personally transformed by this Truth.

Words for Worship 3: Eucharistic Prayer

The Great Thanksgiving Prayer of Cain Our Father

It is truly fitting and right to praise you at all times and in all places, O God, Saviour of the world. For you made all humankind in your own image, to rule your creation in peace, and commanded us to live together in love forever.

And though Cain our father rose in anger and killed his brother, yet you had mercy on him. You gave him a covenant, and marked him with a protecting sign; you placed the gravest sinners beyond human judgment.

With the same steadfast love you led your people Israel out of slavery; and when they deserted you and worshipped false gods – still you did not forsake them. You gave them your law to guide them, and led them through the desert to a new land of promise.

Again, when the people of Nineveh were sunk in wickedness, and the earth could no longer bear their wrongs – even then you did not destroy them. You sent Jonah your prophet to warn them of judgment; and the whole people repented, and changed their ways, and were spared.

So in every place where we made war, you have led us towards peace; where we fell into sin, you forgave us; where we wandered, you called us back with promises of love.

And in due time you sent your Son himself, to seek out the lost and bring them the good news of your boundless mercy. He did not keep himself to the company of the righteous; he chose sinners for his friends; and laying before them your gift of forgiveness, he died for them, showing the fullness of love.

Then you raised him from the dead, and poured out his spirit on humankind, sharing his victory even with those who rejected him. Now we sinners, too, rejoice to give thanks for the death and risen life of your Son; and in the power of his spirit we have turned from our errors to follow his example, and share his saving life in the breaking of bread.

For on the night he was handed over to suffering and death, our Lord Jesus Christ took bread; and when he had given thanks to you, he broke it and gave it to his disciples and said –

'Take, eat: This is my body, which is given for you. Do this in remembrance of me.'

After supper he took the cup of wine; and when he had given thanks, he gave it to them and said –

'Drink of this, all of you: This is my blood of the new covenant, which is shed for you and for many for the forgiveness of sins. Whenever you drink it, do this for the remembrance of me.'

Therefore, Father, of all the things that are yours we offer you these, which are yours especially. We offer them gladly, as he told us, giving thanks for his death and resurrection. And seeing that the power of sin is broken, and Christ is all in all, we praise you and we bless you.

We praise you, we bless you, we give thanks to you, and we pray to you, Lord our God.

Now send your sanctifying spirit, to show us that this bread and this cup are the body and blood of your Son, and every sin is pardoned, and every debt is redeemed, and you have made us your holy people. And bring us at last to his kingdom of peace. Already we gather to welcome him; and lifting our voices with angels and archangels, and with all the company of heaven, we join in the triumphal song:

Holy, holy, holy Lord, God of power and might.
Heaven and earth are full of your glory.
Hosanna in the highest.
                                                         Rick Fabian

7

Belonging, behaving, believing

When entering St Gregory of Nyssa Episcopal Church in San Francisco one is struck by the immediate presence of the altar, close to the entrance, inscribed at its base with the words, 'this guy eats with sinners'. Beyond the table, itself located in a round room with no seating and a beautiful mural of an eclectic variety of saints above, one can see through glass doors to a courtyard where the baptismal 'font' is located; a rock, from which water gently streams. To the right of the altar room is another beautiful space with chairs, a lectern and a preacher's stool. There people gather for listening, learning and prayer.

While really a pre-emergent church, the worship space of St Gregory's physically reflects a major shift in postmodern religious life. The altar is close to the entrance, with nothing blocking access. The font is not at the principal door or in some other way in front of the altar, signalling that Baptism comes before admission to Communion in the life of a believer. Rather, the table is the entry point, and sits alongside the space for teaching, preaching and praying. The font is, in fact, not immediately noticeable. One must look for it and perhaps even seek some clear direction on how to get to Baptism. St Gregory's reflects what emergents live out in their communities: that the development of a faith life is not a series of linear steps beginning with Baptism and ending in full communion with the presence of Christ at Eucharist, but a journey that might just begin at the table – or not.

In seeking to understand the motivation of the liturgical life and flow of emergent churches, one must acknowledge their starting place; what is accepted by emergents without question. Emergent Christians, firmly committed to their faith in Christ, accept that church can no longer be organized in traditional linear fashion: people brought to church for Baptism, raised on weekly worship and Sunday School, approaching Eucharist through appropriate age or Confirmation, proceeding on to marriage and the bringing of children to Baptism to begin the cycle again, with a final exit through burial. This linear, anticipated movement of growing up in the faith no longer prevails in Western culture. Emergents understand that the culture, generally speaking, is no longer Christian and that the church cannot have the same expectations of society as it always has. Likewise, society does not have the same expectations of the church as it once had. Things that were once taken for granted are no longer anticipated milestones of life. This, coupled with the decline of any economic, political or social pressure to be a Christian, means that traditional models of incorporation are no longer effective in many contexts.

In the traditional church this linear path to faith still dominates. It might look to some as if we continue to plan our programme for a past age. This institutional path is characterized by emergents as 'believing, behaving and belonging'; the unspoken understanding that the way life in the inherited church works is that one must believe (or your parents and godparents on your behalf), one must learn to behave and then one will belong. Throughout Christianity, Baptism before being admitted to Communion has been the norm. However, some churches admit children to Communion only after it is determined that they understand what they are doing. To really belong, proper behaviour that reflects a particular understanding must be demonstrated. Our canons and our liturgical texts say that we belong after Baptism, the rite itself, yet this is not truly the case. In the Church of England admission to Communion is normally after episcopal Confirmation, rarely administered before the age of ten, though admission to Communion of children before Confirmation, after preparation, is permitted in most dioceses where the parish has satisfied the bishop that certain requirements are in place. In The Episcopal Church it is most typical that when baptized children can consume solid food then they are given Communion. Some congregations still practise First Communions, particularly in those with Caribbean or Latino cultural composition. Perhaps also reflective of the spoken and unspoken definition of what it means to fully belong is that some churches do not count children in their Sunday worship attendance even if they are receiving communion. It may be that they are not yet considered fully members; they do not yet fully belong, because they are not yet fully grown in the faith by the unspoken standards of a particular congregation. Such linear thinking of faith formation prevails – one belongs when the believing and the behaving is in accordance with particular norms.

Within the inherited church, as well as among emergents, there is an increasing recognition that the pattern of believing, behaving and belonging has become much less predictable and uniform, but there may still be in parts of the inherited church a tendency to assume that it has the power to shape and control the development of the individual's faith life. Emergent Christians suggest that the power to determine one's spiritual life belongs with God and the individual. Emergent liturgical life seeks to make this clear. As in the best of the mainstream churches, through words, gestures and physical space a broad and gracious welcome is clearly articulated to all – no matter where one perceives oneself to be in one's understanding of God or one's own inner life.

Emergents understand the linear path of believing, behaving and belonging as a barrier to the faith development of postmodern people, and they work around it. They reverse the process, creating a new norm of 'belonging, behaving, believing'. 'Showing up' means that you are 'in' and may fully participate in worship – including Eucharist. Baptism or other rites of admission are not required. Behaving and believing are not necessary for being an accepted part of the church, and are understood as part of a process, a journey, that comes along in time through the experience that is inherently offered through full inclusion in the life of the community. Hence, the presence of the altar, almost literally, at the entrance of St Gregory of Nyssa is a bold and divergent statement that all are welcome at the table no matter who they are, what their church experience is or how they might define their faith life at that particular moment in time.

At the Church of the Apostles, during our visit the congregation framed its Lenten worship with the theme of 'Faithful Wandering'. Wandering is considered a good thing in emergent churches. It is all right not to know exactly where you are. In the liturgical texts (fully noted on page 118) one can see that the journey matters and being honest about one's lack of clarity is not just a matter for spiritual direction or private disclosure with a priest or small group, but for the worship and glory of God. The words of welcome included the following:

> Implicit to wandering, though, is the lack of a home, a place in which to settle down and rest in. This is a difficult thing to bear. And though we wander in the ways of God all year round, Lent is a time to reflect on the difficulty of this journey, the less romantic parts of wandering,

the struggle, the hunger, the thirst, the cost of the train fare. Eventually we may find ourselves asking God for a sign that we will indeed arrive. Will we ever get there?

While many people in the general culture no longer respond to the pastoral care of the linear process of faith development traditionally offered by the church, people are spiritually hungry and would like to explore a life with God. Such welcome as that found at the Church of the Apostles articulates, honours and creates necessary communal space for people to belong – even in their unbelieving – so they may explore faith. Peter Rollins, in *How (Not) to Speak of God*, notes:

> In this way the emerging conversation is demonstrating an ability to stand up and engage in a powerless, space-creating discourse that opens up thinking and offers hints rather than orders. In short, the emerging community must endeavour to be a question rather than an answer and an aroma rather than food . . . For too long the Church has been seen as an oasis in the desert – offering water to those who are thirsty. In contrast, the emerging community appears more as a desert in the oasis of life, offering silence, space and desolation amidst the sickly nourishment of Western capitalism. It is in this desert, as we wander together as nomads, that God is to be found. For it is here that we are nourished by our hunger.

When postmoderns come to church perhaps they recognize within themselves spiritual hunger and a need for a purposeful life. They often come with little understanding or articulation of how one nurtures the spiritual life or who God is. They are wandering faithfully, just by being spiritually hungry, but with no common or pervasive framework available to them in the common culture. There are many, many choices. Moot, a London emergent community (see page 130) which seeks to reach the 'never-churched', speaks of itself as offering 'a rhythm' of life for people who may want to be on the Christian spiritual journey, articulating what life looks like for those who have come to 'believe'. Ian Mobsby, in his book *New Monastic Friars*, speaks of Moot's mission in this way:

> In this busy city it is easy to see our Christian spirituality as a part of our life, a Sunday affair. However, as a community, living this rhythm helps us to see God in every moment of life, and to hear the voice of the Spirit beckoning us to come and follow in the footsteps of where God already is at work, beckoning us to join in. In that sense it is

also a call to mission, in bringing the good news to this broken and fragmented world.

Living a rhythm helps us as a community to allow people to shift from being consumers of church, or spiritual tourists, into being pilgrims, and partakers in the body of Christ. It also allows people to easily journey with us, so they can belong without necessarily believing – in that we become a fluid community at the edges with the rhythm at our centre.

An open table where all are welcome to receive Eucharist was a consistent element of emergent churches. It was clear that they understood this to be among the most important messages of belonging. In sacramental worship, the liturgy directs us to full communion with Christ, expressed in the sharing of his presence in bread and wine. Inviting everyone to be part of the Eucharist is seen as one of the essential ways we share who God is in Christ: loving, welcoming and inclusive. For the emergent, to place any barrier there is counterintuitive and counter-productive to the ministry of helping people discover faith. Mark Berry, leader of Safe Space in Telford, England, writes in a guide booklet called *Navigatio*:

> Welcome. The door is open, the table has room, the food is plentiful, the water is cool, the company is warm, the rest is undisturbed, the shelter is total, welcome! There are no special places, there is no head of the table, there are no VIPs, there is no honoured guest, there is no standing, there are no servants, there are no exceptions, welcome. The welcome is universal, the entrance is free, the invitation is open, the hand is extended, there is no time limit, the time is now, the meal is served, welcome. Eat and drink, rest, think, speak, be yourself, be one with us, be one with God, welcome. Whether you deserve it or not, whether you think you deserve it or not, all are welcome, you are welcome, Christ welcomed his brothers and sisters to the table, he washed them as a servant washed important visitors, he fed them as parents feed their children, he laughed with them as friends laugh together, he blessed them as a host blesses guests, he loved them as God loves all creation.

This radical welcome may appeal to those who are accustomed to receiving communion and who are comfortable with it as an inclusive event. For others the Eucharist may be intimidating. There may be a desire to experience 'the aroma and not yet the food' and this may go on for quite some time. A woman from St Gregory of Nyssa in

San Francisco, speaking on the church's 'Dancing with God' DVD, said of her faith journey: 'I couldn't even think about Baptism. It took me months just to receive Communion. I would get close and then I would just not be able to do it. Baptism took me another two years.' In the churches we experienced, there was no pressure to move from belonging on to behaving, let alone believing, within a particular time-frame. Belonging in regular worship could be as far as a person might go, never embracing certain behaviour or traditional Christian belief. This is not an issue for emergents. They understand that they may be a small part of a person's journey, or someone may spend years in that particular community. They do not measure the invitation to belong by a desired outcome but by the welcome they understand Jesus to have offered. Belonging is the beginning.

The faithful wanderer who seeks a deeper life with Christ may want to embrace Christian behaviour and belief, and we experienced creative liturgical gesture and teaching that helped to facilitate this part of the journey. Full inclusion in the behaviour of the worshipping congregation was often accomplished through unspoken rubrics, if you will, with the community itself offering the instruction by their gestures. Sometimes there was careful or even scripted verbal explanation, but the movement of the congregation often provided the cues of what to do next and why. As more fully discussed in Chapters 8 and 9, creative and careful liturgical design assured that this important aspect of corporate speaking, singing, gesture and movement did not disrupt liturgical flow, but rather added content to it. Use of simple chants, responses to prayers and silence helped people engage in corporate prayer and worship. Music that was easy to sing or listen to was prevalent in all the churches we visited and engaged people, as it always does, in a way that the spoken word does not. This is discussed fully in Chapter 10.

The Crossing in Boston accomplished this inclusion exceptionally well, beginning with an explanation of the theme and intention of the worship, inclusive welcome and introduction of leaders. Throughout worship, movement was carried out by the congregation already familiar with the liturgical flow of The Crossing. For example, moving from the early part of the liturgy with the congregation seated on pillows or in chairs in front of the altar, to standing in a circle, inclusive of the altar and president, was accomplished while singing a simple chant, everyone moving the seats out of the way to accommodate our change of posture. No verbal instruction was given. Those in the congregation already familiar with the gesture of preparation for communion initiated movement, and newcomers naturally followed. It was easy to discern what to do next simply by moving with the gesture of the body. This was well done also at St Paul's Seattle, as will be further described in Chapter 9.

St Gregory of Nyssa employed dance and procession to move the congregation from one room to another, from one liturgical action to another. Behaviour was introduced with easy movement in which a newcomer could be quickly embraced and liturgically competent. The Eucharist at St Gregory's, which takes place with people standing as a crowd around the table, is carried out by eucharistic ministers (including children), person to person in a random fashion, sharing the bread and wine with all who want to receive communion.

For the reception of communion, as noted, an inclusive welcome was issued in every case where it was part of the liturgy. Instructions were given or gestured as to how the bread and wine might be received in a particular setting. All in all, while local practice varied, emergent churches had in common a culture of sensitive and pastoral liturgical planning that anticipated the needs of worshippers new to the Christian life.

We experienced corporate behaviour and the theology conveyed through the liturgy as easy to pick up in emergent churches, and could see how this contributed to a deeper sense of belonging. Likewise, it encouraged participation in liturgical behaviour that allowed people new to the faith to engage in what believing Christians say and do. Liturgy, rather than a measure of what one knows and already believes, might be seen as a sort of practice for the Christian life, a way of 'trying on' the faith, so to speak. Emergent churches allow believing and behaving to meld together over time. Phyllis Tickle notes: 'As behaviour begins to condition living, it also begins to shape belief until the two become one.'

Within liturgy itself, the concept of Open Space was employed as a means of belief exploration. This occurred in place of a traditional sermon where one seminary-trained ordained person might preach a sermon, with a clear agenda of what was to be understood from the Scriptures of the day. When traditional sermons were preached, there was always a time for the congregation to respond to what had been taught. As was the case with Moot and several other congregations, there were non-worship gatherings for theological discussion, some-times called 'theology pubs'. Socializing, eating and drinking were accompanied by serious theological conversations. The intent of such formats is to create space for personal exploration and reflection on the themes of the day or appointed topics of interest, and to give voice to anyone who wants to participate in the faith conversation.

We experienced four churches that were as concerned as others with the individual spiritual life but in a way that did not frame the journey in the context of the Eucharist. Leaders, however, articulated important and worthy pastoral reasons for not being eucharistic com-munities. For example, at Thad's in Los Angeles we were told that leadership had discussed this as part of its identity development, but they perceived that people 'worked against the liturgy and so moved away from it'. Jimmy Bartz, pastor and priest of Thad's, indicated that they had the Eucharist about once a quarter using the liturgy of The Episcopal Church. But he stated, 'We don't always have Communion, but we always have communion.' We were not sure we felt included in that. However, members of Thad's expressed a deep and genuine sense of bonding, one to another, through a common journey of faith discovery and the creating of church. Ethos @ St Nick's functions as a service supplemental to a primary eucharistic service and is intended to explore the spiritual life in other ways.

Anglican liturgy intends to convey the faith in both form and content. From our perspective, eucharistic communities have a different sense of communion from those who do not have this as the centrepiece of liturgy. It is not that the teaching of the non-eucharistic communities lacks orthodoxy, but because there is no regular movement towards the high point of the Eucharist and the focus is typically geared towards the nurture and healing of the individual spiritual life, the doctrinal content for Christian believing occurs only in the locally designed preaching or ritual and in the prayers. Sacramental churches will by nature have more doctrinal teaching since they include and make use of authorized liturgy or at least its form. Eucharistic liturgy neces-sarily provides a framework that is objective and connected to the wider body of the church, and will frame the process of belonging, behaving and believing differently from a non-sacramental church.

Emergent churches do make available Baptism and Confirmation, but again there is no prescribed time-frame for these rituals that move the Christian life beyond the worship setting. Social outreach was at least a small part of most of the congregations we visited, and Christians both traditional and emergent would agree that serving the world is an important part of everyday faith life. We heard almost nothing in worship about what Christian moral behaviour might look like in a particular community. Some communities had detailed 'rules of life', where values and modelling for Christian living were explained as that community understood it, and people were invited to participate. *Life Together in the Way of Jesus*, a rule of life for the Church of the Apostles, notes the following:

> 'Life Together' is a description of our community 'praxis' (of the kind of life we are seeking to lead in the way of Jesus) rather than a set of beliefs or doctrines (as with most catholic Christians, our beliefs are summarized in the ecumenical Nicene creed). At Church of the Apostles we are 'students of Jesus', who are being shown and taught how to live his way of being in the world, so that the truth of our faith is expressed less in 'what' we believe (concepts, ideas, doctrines) and more centered around 'whom' we follow and pattern our lives upon. We are putting front and center the direct call of Jesus upon our lives, through the Gospels, and in the power of the Spirit to a 'new way of life' that Jesus intends for his followers.

The Church of the Apostles' rule reads:

- Love God and love neighbors.
- Give invitations and provide welcome.
- Engage community and practice faith.
- Share stories and throw parties.
- Create art and exchange gifts.
- Renew culture and steward creation.

Moot publishes a similar rule, and as noted it is called a rhythm. Ian Mobsby describes this in his book *New Monastic Friars*:

> We live the moot rhythm of life through presence, acceptance, creativity, balance, accountability and hospitality . . . A rhythm of life should be exactly that, a rhythm, not a full concerto with every instrument written up, but rather the background beat that keeps everything else in order, that calls things back on track when they deviate, that reminds us of the type of music we are wanting to play, or perhaps more accurately, what type of lifestyles we are wanting to lead.

One can see in these expanded and distinct modes, perhaps, the 'commissioning' of the baptismal liturgy. 'Rule of life' language may make sense for a person new to the faith, who may need to spend time living it before committing to it. This process of 'trying on' may or may not lead to Baptism or the deeper commitment of Confirmation. Some emergent churches do emphasize Confirmation but in general it seemed less important than the development of the faith journey and participation in the local community.

Faith development is very important to emergent leaders, but they separate commitment to Christ from commitment to the institution of the church. One outcome is that in general, they do not express much concern for the long-term sustainability of their congregations. We spoke with several leaders who were not worried in the same way as a congregation with older, more heavily invested parishioners would be about whether their congregations would exist in five years' time. Longevity of the congregation itself was not part of the agenda of providing faith development for the spiritually hungry postmodern generation. Getting them fed – today – seemed of prime importance. Given the age group, it is reasonable to assume that someone in their 20s or 30s may not be a 'member' of a congregation in five years, and so a lack of membership pressure seems age-appropriate in these congregations. But also, culturally, emergent leaders lack a 'believer' agenda that must be met. When we spoke with Jonathan Myers, a new church planter in the Diocese of Olympia, his view was that 'the emerging movement is something that may exist for a time, in order to stimulate creativity, to do what the Spirit wants, and then to die'. In other words, an end-product of belief is not tied up with institutional sustainability, of building a sure future for those to come after current leaders and members have moved on.

Whether an emergent community is sacramental or not, it is characteristic of them all that the process of belonging, behaving and believing is what creates church. Emergents understand this to be their reason for being. Perhaps, eventually, committed Christians are born from this non-linear process and then engage with the task of joining in the articulation of the local ecclesial identity to the wider community. Faith formation through liturgy will impact the outcome, should a person choose a deeper engagement with the faith. In the meantime, though, all shall be welcome and included in its development and exercise, given the freedom to move at a pace determined by the individual wandering faithfully with the Holy Spirit.

Worshipping communities 4: St Paul's Church Seattle
Seattle – 28 February 2010

St Paul's, Roy St, Seattle is not an emergent church. We include it here for contrast, but also because in the midst of a pilgrimage taking us to emergent churches we found in this Episcopal church worship that swept us off our feet and modelled what we might hope for in many more churches across our Communion.

St Paul's describes itself as 'an accepting, progressive Anglo-Catholic parish renewing its people for their Christian lives in today's world through worship, spiritual formation, engagement with the arts, life in community, and acts of compassion'. The rector is the Reverend Melissa Skelton (known as Mother Melissa). The liturgy used is the most common eucharistic rite in the Book of Common Prayer of The Episcopal Church, with a huge commitment to the spirituality of the rite and the participation of the congregation.

It has no claim to be an emerging church and its Sunday Eucharist is not 'alternative', though it does run its own alternative worship on Sunday evenings. We went because it had been recommended to us and we had a free Sunday morning. We did not go to it planning to include it in our research, but the liturgy was so stunning that we felt it needed to be written up, if only to stand alongside the emerging church material, drawing out both similarities and differences.

The church is a post-war concrete edifice, high and simple inside, a church typical of the mid-twentieth-century liturgical movement, which introduced an austerity where the eye is drawn to the altar, though the seating here was conventional in terms of benches in rows facing the altar.

We shared in the Sunday Mass there on 28 February 2010, the Second Sunday of Lent. The Lent emphasis was strong. There was a congregation of about 150, with a wide age range, including a large proportion of young adults. The presider and preacher was one of the associate priests. The rector assisted him, along with a deacon. The only microphone was on the lectern for the first two readings and the sermon. There was a choir of about a dozen adults, sitting in the gallery, leading the singing in such a way that the congregation was supported but the choir did not stand out. There was a printed programme of the 'running order' for the service, together with the use of the Prayer Book and *The Hymnal*. The Sunday sheet included this sentence (quoted earlier, in Chapter 4): 'If you are unfamiliar with the ritual customs of The Episcopal Church, simply relax with the liturgy and let the rest of the congregation carry you in worship.'

Much of the liturgy that morning we describe in Chapter 9. It began with a processional entry, which effectively gathered the community and created unity. It moved through a substantial penitential rite (including the Decalogue and the Trisagion ('Holy God and holy strong, have mercy upon us') to a Liturgy of the Word, where every element – reading, psalm, reading, sequence hymn, Gospel and sermon – was presented with care and clarity. The ministers remained entirely focused on the Scripture and the reader. We sang the Creed, noting that some used the pronoun 'she' of the Holy Spirit. The Prayers of the People were a sung litany from the Prayer Book, with spoken additional intercessions by members of the congregation and a concluding collect sung by the presider.

The Peace led into the Eucharist, with procession of the elements, censing of the gifts, singing of much of the Eucharistic Prayer, slow intentional gestures and a beautiful distribution with real prayerfulness. The liturgy also ended relationally, the congregation turning towards the ministers at the door for the Dismissal.

Repeatedly through the service we were invited to keep a time of 'silence and stillness'. The St Paul's website (<www.StPaulseattle.org>) explains the silence in this way:

> A significant part of our worship is punctuation of the liturgy with periods of silence. Our brief, or sometimes lingering, moments of silence focus our attention on the present and what is taking place in the present, rather than rush to the next thing. We listen, we engage, we reflect, we move on, we stay grounded. These moments of participatory silence are not dead space; they are very much alive. We are a people, who by drenching ourselves in the treasures of the sacraments, draw together in fellowship to contemplate, to be sustained, renewed, and inspired, and to worship a loving God.

In Chapter 9 we analyse the effectiveness of worship at St Paul's in terms of the deep spirit of engagement by the congregation, the well-developed sense of appropriate pace and the beautiful and inclusive action and gesture in which all were caught up. They lived out their claim to be 'deeply committed to the beauty and profundity of the rituals, readings, prayers and symbolic actions known as the liturgy'.

8

Text or typikon

Ethos @ St Nick's in Portsmouth might be described as an alternative worship service seeking to become an emergent church. It displays three key characteristics of emergent church worship: a desire to establish a satisfying liturgical order and shape that can genuinely lead people into worship, an intention to create strong and beautiful texts and a reticence about requiring people to respond from the standpoint of faith.

On the occasion of our visit on 7 February 2010, the theme of the worship was 'The face of God'. The shape of the liturgy was this:

Music and both words and images, that might describe God, on
    the screen
Greeting
Exploration of belief
    An extended introduction spoken by Bev
    A simple form of stations looking at and choosing images of
        God
    A profound unscripted meditation
Texts including Scripture (Psalm 139)
Scripted meditations
Prayer

The two later meditations are those printed on pages 45–6. They were written specifically for that liturgy by Bev Robertson, the parish priest. They have the beauty of poetry and the freshness of creative theology.

But the interest lies also in the shape of the liturgy. To be honest, it was quite difficult initially to feel that we were engaged in worship. At least the first third of the service presented negative pictures of God, some fairly austere or even frightening (none of them obviously Jesus, except a raw crucifixion), some representations of hell, mixed in with images of natural disasters, while passages were read that described or conjured up pictures of an unattractive God obsessed with sin and punishment. Devoting ten minutes or so to projecting a false picture of God, in order to knock it down, was a challenge within a kind of worshipping atmosphere in a sacred space. But Bev Robertson's meditation moved it into worship, some of the later texts made that more explicit and when we reached the words 'Let us pray', they felt entirely appropriate. We had been taken on a journey and it had brought us into a place of prayer.

The approach used that evening at Ethos @ St Nick's reflects one of the concerns of the emergent church: to help people let go of theologies that have left them puzzled, wounded and angry. Many who find their way into the emergent churches come with the baggage of bad experience of church and of narrow, life-denying theologies. We found this especially true in England, where some fresh expression communities have emerged in reaction to some evangelical approaches. Where we found that to be the case, those who devise worship will sometimes want to create liturgies that only turn into worship when some of the negativities have been explored and laid aside. They will also sometimes want to create liturgies where people can listen, explore, think their own thoughts and not be asked to speak or sing at all. At Ethos @ St Nick's, though the occasion was experienced as worshipful, the only invitation to do something that required a response of faith was to pray and the only oral contribution to that for the community was to speak an 'Amen'. Interestingly Bev has some reservations about the word 'worship'. 'Nobody,' she says, 'uses it outside the church, at least not in a positive way.' What she wants to do is to 'create a sense of the sacred'. It is interesting, she suggests, that when people speak of the church building as a sacred space they are normally speaking of an empty building. Our task, she believes, is to create worship (if we use that word) that engenders a sense of the sacred in a building where a community has gathered.

Some of those same suspicions of traditional church were to be found in New York at Transmission. As quoted earlier, Bowie Snodgrass speaks of people in their 20s needing to 'reconstitute themselves, as if they were shipwrecked and needed to put out their oar and row to solid shore'. The liturgy in which we shared had this shape:

Psalm 63 – spoken by a single reader with sung response by all
Three readings, one from Isaiah, one from Mark's Gospel, one
    from a non-biblical source
Homily
Ritual (described in Chapter 9) – with a hymn within it
Closing song

Once again there was a clear shape and development, and in this setting there was active participation both in a ritual action and also in
singing, but there was no prayer. It felt like a gathering of serious
people of enquiry and of faith, but because of its shape and structure
it never quite felt like worship. These were people on a journey; it
was a journey they clearly wanted to bring them closer to God. Although not on the occasion we were there, sometimes they would
have Communion in a simple form, without an ordained minister.
On Ash Wednesday, we shared supper, but it was very clearly after
rather than part of the liturgy.

'The Table', which is the Thursday night gathering of the Safe Space
community in Telford, is in much the same place. Its meeting for
Communion is, as at Transmission, in a private home. Ten men and
women gathered together in fellowship that evening, but this is only
part of what this community, which regards itself as missional, is
engaged in. Their liturgy to equip them for 'a liturgy of service' in
the community proceeded like this:

A simple meal around the dining table
An informal homily
Scripted prayer (set out below)
Psalm (130)
The words of institution of Jesus at the Last Supper
The sharing of the bread and wine
A post-Communion text based on John 3.16
A labyrinth experience (described on page 103)

Here, at Ethos @ St Nick's, Transmission and Safe Space, are honest
and successful attempts to explore how liturgy may serve the needs
of those who are on a journey. They are exceedingly carefully prepared,
often devised by the whole group or by several members of it. They
have a logic, shape and development of their own. They move people
in a faith direction. They employ Scripture. They value fellowship.

They share ideas. Sometimes they are drawn into prayer and into worship. They feel related to the liturgy of the church, but remain something a little different.

They are not, however, what we encountered in most of the emergent churches. What we found in most of them was much more connected with the liturgy of the wider Church, eucharistic worship, following very clearly the normative shape and structure of the Eucharist, and, alongside creative texts of their own, also using very freely and frequently material from the authorized liturgies of the Church of England and The Episcopal Church. Other than Transcendence, which used only authorized material, we found that the emergent churches were more interested in keeping with the shape of the mainstream liturgy than with its words, and we found a good deal of creativity by talented wordsmiths with sophisticated theological skills.

The Church of the Apostles uses The Episcopal Church's Rite 3, which is an outline rite without texts. While it is not intended for use at the main Sunday celebration, COTA uses it in this way with the bishop's dispensation. Karen Ward views the Book of Common Prayer of The Episcopal Church as a *typikon* (in the Orthodox churches a book of liturgical directives and rubrics): not necessarily using the words, but always the shape. She understands liturgical language to be a distinctive language different from both conversation and written communication. It requires resonance, rhythm and sometimes capacity to be used repeatedly. The designers of liturgy at COTA are taught the formula, of how a collect, for instance, is patterned, and then allowed to create it. So authorized texts are sources, as well as in use themselves.

There are five stages in the eucharistic liturgy about which it is important to describe emergent church practice.

The first is Welcome. The liturgical provision in official rites is minimal, sometimes no more than a formal greeting, with perhaps an informal word of welcome to follow. The emergent churches attach huge importance to welcome, as for instance the text by Mark Berry of Safe Space (Chapter 7, page 73) makes clear. At St Gregory of Nyssa all those with any kind of ministerial role in the service are given these written instructions:

> The crucial practice for all participants in the liturgy is prayerful atten-
> tion; that is watching the entire liturgy with an eye to the whole action.

The core value of the liturgy is glorifying the stranger through clear, direct, warm invitation, thus making it possible for new-comers, old-timers, children and adults to participate fully. Jesus welcomes everyone to his table, act like you mean it!

At Moot there are refreshments on arrival because 'all our services begin with relational time'. Then follows the Invocation, which on 14 March 2010 was this:

We meet in the name of God the Creator, the God who sent the Redeemer into the needs of our world. We meet in the name of the Redeemer, who with the interaction of the Creator and Spirit, brought liberation and reconciliation between all matter and the divine. We meet in the name of the Companion, who sustains all life and freedom, both inner and outer.
We meet in the name of the Creator, Redeemer and Companion.   Ian Mobsby

At COTA the 'Opening Words' was a scene-setting piece, with a recorded male voice and a video of roads, travel and subways to illustrate the 'Faithful Wanderers' theme of the day. It ended, 'So step aboard and journey with us, here, in the shadow of the Almighty and listen for what the Spirit is saying to God's people. Welcome to the Church of the Apostles.'

The second is Penitence, where we find the widest variation of practice. There were some emergent churches where confession seemed not to be part of the worship, even in Lent, though there were others that explained that because it was Lent there was an emphasis on penitence that might not always be present. There was no element of penitence (whether penitence for corporate or personal sin) in four of the churches (including the highly liturgical St Gregory of Nyssa, unless the Trisagion – 'Holy God, holy and strong, holy and immortal, have mercy on us' – could be said to provide that element). But in all the other communities there were prayers of penitence, though only at The Crossing and at Blesséd was the word 'sin' used.

At The Crossing we were invited by three voices, speaking from within the 'congregation', to reflect and make confession, and then we said together an authorized text of The Episcopal Church:

God of all mercy, we confess that we have sinned against you, opposing your will in our lives. We have denied your goodness in each other, in ourselves, and in the world you have created. We repent of the evil that enslaves us, the evil we have done, and the evil done on our behalf. Forgive, restore and strengthen us through our Saviour Jesus Christ, that we may abide in your love and serve only your will.

At COTA we said a confession, antiphonally, reading from the screen, though it was not called a confession but an 'affirmation'. At Safe Space a single voice prayed:

Forgive us Lord for not taking the time to know you more,
Forgive us Lord for not taking the time to know each other more,
Forgive us Lord for not taking the time to know your world more.

At Blesséd in Gosport the penitential rite included a video, a ritual with stones (described in Chapter 9) and a Kyrie. At Transmission, though there were no words of penitence, the Lenten ritual could be made a form of confession by those who wanted to.

At Thad's, as part of the 'Prayers of the People', which were not only intercessory, a leader prayed these clauses, each followed by a significant time of silence and a response: 'God of Love, we know that you hear us.'

We gather with one another and with you and acknowledge to you and to one another that our thoughts, words, action and inaction have not always been in line with your Loving Way.
At times we have not been good listeners. We have failed to serve, been quick to criticize, and inflexible in our judgements of others and ourselves.
We have been angry and frustrated with our own brothers and sisters, your beloved creatures. At times we are self-indulgent, vain, envious.
For all false judgements, for uncharitable thoughts towards our neighbors, and for our prejudice and contempt toward those who differ from us, accept our sincere desire to reform our thought and action, our hearts.   Quinton Peeples

At Compline at St Mark's Cathedral in Seattle, just as the congregation heard but did not join in with the Creed, so also they heard but did not speak the confession, and with it an absolution.

Absolution is another matter. We heard words of absolution only at Transcendence, St Paul's Church and St Mark's Cathedral in Seattle, Blesséd and Moot. There seems to be an understanding in some of the emergent churches that absolution comes in the very act of confessing and that a formal priestly absolution has no function. Not surprisingly it is the churches with the strongest catholic tradition that retain an absolution. Ian Mobsby at Moot was surprised that so few emergent churches included it. In his community people had asked for it and regarded it as important. Clearly, how postmodern young people experience a sense of sinfulness, make confession and experience a sense of release, healing and forgiveness is something with which the emergent churches are engaging. At Moot some were unable to cope with the traditional words of the Agnus Dei – 'Lamb of God, you take away the sin of the world'. Instead they sing 'Lamb of God, you take away the *selfishness* of the world.'

It was obvious that the theological message of emergent churches was above all else of a loving and forgiving God, known in Jesus Christ, who very much wants a connection with individuals. Some of the communities we visited were clear that their particular audience needed healing from past traumatic experiences of church, or affirmation because of their particular life situation. At Thad's, for instance, a church which attracts people in the highly competitive entertainment industry, the leadership seeks to create a very affirming and positive environment. Jimmy Bartz, their priest and pastor, notes: 'In the entertainment industry, there is rejection after rejection, perhaps then some excitement, then rejection again. People need affirming.' At Thad's the theme in Lent was, as already mentioned, 'Your baggage – God's got it', a hopeful message intended to convey God's love and concern for individuals and their burdens.

The third area is Intercession. In a number of communities we were surprised to find communal intercession excluded. It was, in just a few places, as if the world outside did not exist. But, of course, intercession is another use of Open Space. Often the stations within it are called 'prayer stations' and nearly always one or more of them focuses on the needs of the world. At Home in Oxford we were invited to 'come and light a taper to make a personal response to what you have heard and to pray for the needs of the world or to offer your personal needs to God'. At Transcendence one of the prayer stations was a multi-media invitation to intercessory prayer for the world with images of devastation and with the song written for the Haiti earthquake appeal. At The Crossing, while gathered around the altar just before the Eucharistic Prayer, there was intercessory prayer 'for ourselves, for our communities, for our world', various people spontaneously speaking out as they were moved, and at points we repeated after the cantor, 'Kyrie, eleison, Christe, eleison'.

At St Gregory of Nyssa, after the greeting of the Gospel book by all, we sang the Lord's Prayer and there then followed Prayers of Intercession, controlled gently by a deacon, with people speaking out their prayers from their seats. Deacons ensured that there was breadth to the prayers, by adding in petitions for missing areas of concern. The presider brought the prayers to their conclusion by singing a collect. At St Paul's Seattle the Prayers of the People were a litany sung by a deacon, with spoken additional intercessions by the congregation and, again, a concluding collect sung by the presider.

At the Church of the Apostles the intercession was incorporated into the Eucharistic Prayer. At Blesséd there was visual intercession material on the screen, including everyone from the victims of the Haitian earthquake to the Archbishop of Canterbury, with an invitation to let the images lead you into prayer.

Although some emergent churches did not include intercession and others made it simply an option within Open Space, others did give intercession prominence and engaged with it in an imaginative way, not least through visual images and music.

Fourth, there is the issue of Eucharistic Prayers. Only Transcendence, Blesséd, Moot and St Paul's Seattle used an authorized prayer in its entirety. At COTA there was a modified version of The Episcopal Church's Prayer A.

Home used a fine Eucharistic Prayer from Steven Shakespeare's *Prayers for an Inclusive Church*. At The Crossing, when it was 'time to gather at God's table, remember Jesus, share the holy meal and receive the blessing of the Holy Spirit', Stephanie Spellers prayed an extemporary Eucharistic Prayer, rich and resonant in its language, with preface, institution narrative, prayer for the Spirit, doxology and Amen. What was missing in terms of a conventional Eucharistic Prayer was any oral participation by the community. Instead we were engaged by gesture, with arms uplifted throughout, except at the epiclesis where we all extended hands towards the elements. At St Gregory of Nyssa a Eucharistic Prayer written by Richard Fabian was used, 'The

Great Thanksgiving Prayer of Our Father Cain' (see page 67). Overall these were full, rich, beautiful and orthodox, but unofficial Eucharistic Prayers, making for joyful and engaging celebration.

Most emergent churches make much of their missional thrust. It was interesting to see how they engaged with the final stage of the Eucharist, with its emphasis on sending out and living the gospel in the world.

At Home the congregation prayed together:

> You are God's servants gifted with dreams and visions
> upon you rests the grace of God like flames of fire;
> love and serve the Lord in the strength of the Spirit;
> may the deep peace of Christ be with you
> the strong arms of God sustain you
> and the power of the Holy Spirit strengthen you
> in every way. Amen.   Diane Karay Tripp

After this there was a conventional blessing and dismissal.

At Blesséd the service ended with a Commission to the congregation and the words, 'The mass is ended. The mission has begun.' At Thad's there was the exchange of the Peace. In most communities the service concluded with a classical Blessing and Dismissal, though at COTA, reflecting the theme of the week, the Dismissal was 'Go, in peace. Wander faithfully.'

At Moot this was the Blessing:

> Get up.
> Do not be afraid,
> Journey with and after God.
> Take up your cross,
> Take strength for the journey,
> Take comfort for your pain,
> Take inspiration from one another,
> Take peace and hope into the world.
> Listen for God in the world,
> the great deep resonance of God with you,
> Always with you, alongside you, before you and ahead of you,
> The constant source of life, the all in all.
> And the blessing of God, Almighty,
> the Creator, Redeemer and Sustainer,

be amongst you and remain with you now and always.
Go in the peace of Christ.
Thanks be to God. Ian Mobsby

Mission and outreach between worship services varied by congregation. Transmission acknowledged that they had lost a former rhythm of worship and outreach to the wider community, having done very public Easter services in bars and other events geared towards reaching the spiritually hungry who had no association with church. The Crossing publicized outreach projects that members could be involved in that were relevant to the local community and initiated by those concerned in the congregation. It seemed that the eucharistic communities were more naturally focused on mission and outreach beyond the gathering for liturgy and worship. While all were focused on the spiritual journey, non-eucharistic communities may be more theologically introspective and less outward focused in orientation, serving the purpose of healing and transformation of the inner life. Thad's and Ethos @ St Nick's were examples of this; the worship was itself an outreach to those in need of affirmation, love and inclusion for an experience of wholeness. The wider concerns of the world were not primary in these contexts.

This is a matter of focus and emphasis. At Safe Space, the opposite could be found. Mark Berry offered during a homily the following as a way of linking liturgy and the work of the church as the active presence of Christ transforming the world:

> Liturgy (the Eucharist) is always the entrance into the presence of the triune God and always ends with the community being sent forth in God's name to transform the world in God's image. Mission is conceived, in other words, as 'the liturgy after the liturgy', the natural consequence of entering into the divine presence in worship.

After the homily, prayer continued, with music in the background, written by Mark for the occasion. The following words made up part of the Eucharistic Prayer:

> The liturgy after the liturgy.
> There is no breathing out without breathing in,
> There is no flow without ebb,
> There is no outpouring without drinking deep of life.

We cannot be love for the community without being drawn
　　deeper ourselves into God,
We cannot bring change to the world without our lives being
　　realigned,
We cannot forgive each other without knowing the freedom of
　　forgiveness ourselves.

We ache for the loneliness of the world and are known by a God
　　who is family,
We cry for a world trapped in greed and are loved by a God
　　who gave up everything,
We fight against a world of little justice and are embraced by a
　　God of mercy.

Forgive us Lord for not taking the time to know you more,
Forgive us Lord for not taking the time to know each other
　　more,
Forgive us Lord for not taking the time to know your world
　　more.

Whether the focus is inward or outward, emergent churches do not
hold as their first matter of importance the survival of the church.
They are concerned with the well-being of the people who come
to be fed, and/or those in the wider community who are in need.
This distinguishes them from many institutional churches who are
primarily concerned with their own survival, and only secondarily
with the spiritually hungry, or those otherwise in need.

As has already been said, there is a wide spectrum in terms of oral
participation in the worship of the emergent churches we visited,
from places where the community simply looks and listens and
invitations to speak and sing are rare, to places where there is much
congregational singing and chanting (discussed in Chapter 10) and
where the entire community says together some of the prayers that
traditionally are reserved to the presiding minister – the collect and
the blessing, for instance. In a world where choral speaking is as
counter-cultural as choral singing, these communities have differed
in whether they think this instance of being counter-cultural is
sufficiently important to persevere. And some, of course, have found
that the sense of community participation is achieved more by

common action and gesture than by words, as the following chapter will explore.

Meanwhile, the final insight on words needs to be not about the words of the liturgy, but about the words that help the initiated to be caught up in the celebration. This can be by rubrics that put people at their ease and encourage a sense of inclusion, and in general the emergent churches seem to have given more attention and priority to these than many other churches. But it is a traditional church that, to our mind, gave the very best message. It is sufficiently good to be worth repeating. 'If you are unfamiliar with the ritual customs of The Episcopal Church,' the service sheet at St Paul's Seattle said, 'simply relax with the liturgy and let the rest of the congregation carry you in worship.' And they did!

Words for worship 4: Songs

Broken

You are broken, I am broken, everyone is broken
You are broken, I am broken, intimately broken

Stay, there is peace beyond anguish
life beyond death, love beyond fear
and we all have to suffer to enter our glory.

Bless, bless and do not curse.
Pull brokenness far from the shadow of curse
put it under the light of the blessing.

Praise, praise to you Lord
for I never realized
broken glass could shine so brightly.

Tara Ward

Given

We may be little, insignificant in the eyes of this world,
but when we realize that God has sent us to the world
   as blessed
our lives will multiply and grow to fill the needs of
   others.
Our gift is not what we can do but who we are.

Who can we be for each other?
Who can we be for the world?
Who can we be for each other?
Lord, who can we be?

How different would our lives be if we believed every
   single gesture;
every act of faith or love or joy or peace or word of
   forgiveness
would multiply as long as there are people to receive it.
Our gift is not what we can do but who we are.

We are given. We are given. We are given.
(We are given. Our gift is who we are. It's who we are!)
Our gift is not what we can do but who we are.

Tara Ward and Ryan Marsh

9

Ritual, gesture, stillness and warm bread

Although discussion of shape and text is important, since emergent churches take great care with both, we are dealing with communities where all the senses are important and the word – spoken, heard and seen – is only part of the picture. Equally so are ritual, symbol, icon and gesture. This is unsurprising, both because that reflects a redis-covery of such things even in our secular culture and also because, of all churches, these are the ones that dig deep into the ancient traditions in order to find what might speak to people today and tomorrow.

We have made reference already to Karen Ward's concept of the 'little altars' (see page 64), the opportunities to discover the images and ideas that attract people within the liturgy and within the physical space in which it is set. The Open Space experience gives participants an opportunity to engage in that way.

But the one altar/little altars issue goes beyond questions of physical space. The liturgical movement at its most focused was an abandon-ment of complexity and a return to simplicity. The liturgy must not be over-fussy. The symbolic action must be bold and clear. People must be engaged in one unitive liturgy, with clear direction and intel-ligible meaning. But the postmodern mind responds to a complex multi-layered liturgy in which the variety of possibility allows people to find that to which they respond positively. Clearly such an approach has both its strengths and its weaknesses. In some ways it seems to represent a strong challenge to the whole direction of liturgical reform in Anglicanism, as well as in the Roman Catholic Church, in the last 50 years. Liturgists have consistently sought to streamline the liturgy and to make its signs and symbols simple, bold and clear. Pastors have worked with people who have often understood the liturgy in a rather privatized way ('making *my* communion') to have a stronger sense of the corporate and the community.

The challenge that the emergent church movement throws down is whether we should be ready to return to complexity. It is fraught with danger, though less so when the context is eucharistic. For when it is, the scattering through the building in a personal exploration or the engagement with many layers of symbol by the individual in their own way is halted and brought together by the return to the corporate as the community gathers, perhaps to exchange the greeting of peace, certainly to gather around the table.

At Transcendence the end of the prayer stations was signalled by the ringing of the bell summoning people back into community. At The Crossing a chant brought us back together and we found ourselves, without announcement or fuss, moved into one large circle around the altar, with excess furniture skilfully and quietly removed. There was also a delightful complexity at St Gregory of Nyssa. At any given moment there were usually several things happening – visual, verbal, processional – and this was not a case of unthinking overloading, but an intentional multi-layering of the liturgy.

It is helpful now to move from this rich, ordered, formal eucharistic world to something very different. On Ash Wednesday evening, sharing in the fortnightly meeting of Transmission in quite a small New York apartment, we were drawn into what was called a 'ritual'.

On the table was an empty glass bowl. The three readings that we heard when the liturgy began were read from texts handwritten on floral pressed paper. After each reading the paper was screwed up and placed in the bowl. In her thoughtful homily Katie Everett invited us to write down some thoughts about our hopes and expectations in the days of Lent, repeatedly saying the things 'we might reflect on in our ten minutes in the shower in the morning'. We spent some time writing and then screwed up our papers and placed them in the bowl, where now a fire had been lit, burning the readings. Some people took a long time and wrote a lot. Ash got made! We sang a Lent hymn from *The Hymnal* and then we made soap. We first made containers for the soap and then the soap itself – from olive oil, goats' milk, honey, herbs and ash, to some extent making our own choices as to what ingredients to include. Then the soap was left to set. The intention was to use the soap each day. It was not spelled out what connection, if anything in particular, was to be made between the using of the soap and the content of the worship. We were called back together (although some continued in the soap-making activity), and Katie led us in the singing of a three-part song. This brought the worship to an end.

In conversation, Bowie Snodgrass confirmed for us that the design of the worship and the ritual in particular was not that the worshipper should be led towards a particular theme or experience, but simply that 'something', undetermined, 'might' happen. It clearly was a setting in which people could explore their personal spiritual journey rather than a corporate one. The implication of this for us was that the image of God was highly individualistic, not necessarily corporate, a rather different experience of God from that which we witness in the Scriptures.

For Transmission what really mattered clearly was the ritual. The Transmission website has a ritual guide by Isaac Everett. 'Ritual,' Bowie Snodgrass told us, 'is the point of the evening.' But we had to learn that the word ritual is being understood in a way different from its mainstream liturgical use. There is not the sense that it has particular truth or grace to convey, nor is there the sense that it is something that by regular repetition will go deeper. Instead ritual is defined simply by the fact that 'something is happening' and its purpose is to provide a non-verbal impetus to thought and reflection. The meaning is entirely subjective. Thus, for instance, though the soap made partly from ash might for some relate to the cleansing from sin element of Lent, for others it might be a daily recalling in the shower of the intentions written down on Ash Wednesday, and for others it might mean something entirely different. To associate ritual, in their sense, as related to symbol is therefore unhelpful.

It is equally unhelpful to relate ritual, as they understood it, as iconic. They understood ritual as something intended to have meaning extracted from it. Iconic suggests that meaning is found by going beyond, more deeply, through the image into the mystery of God where, yes, 'something will happen'. The something is not prescribed *per se* in distinction from the teaching of the church that would suggest that when one is open to the transcendent God, the 'something' will be of God, albeit a mystery. We did not sense that it was expected, or even hoped for, that the 'something' would come from God. In our own experience and understanding of church as corporate and of God as Trinity, these would be important elements of worship.

We had a concern about ritual that might convey an unintended negative meaning. Specifically, what did burning the papers on which the Scriptures were written mean? Later we thought perhaps it was about ensuring that the word of Scripture found its way into the soap that would be used through Lent. Furthermore Katie had carefully written the Scriptures and readings on fine paper, which seemed an important part of her personal offering, and symbolic for her as the leader of the ritual. We could receive this as a gift – and certainly, we needed ashes! But it remained an odd aspect of the ritual if one was looking through conventional liturgical eyes searching for symbolic meaning.

There was, even in the constricted space of the apartment, some freedom for people to do their own thing, to pursue their own journey. This manifested itself, for instance, in some people continuing to make soap right to the end of the ritual instead of rejoining the group for the final song. We learned that on some occasions there would be rather more of that sort of individualism, especially when there were stations to explore.

In this way, while our own desire to engage in a particular way would have not been appropriate (for example, wanting to say an extemporaneous prayer of thanksgiving at the end of the evening), it did seem that all sorts of non-verbal activity were acceptable. This underlined the message of identity and intent: that Transmission has as a value the pre-eminence of the personal spiritual journey over the concept of the body of Christ gathered as one, journeying together as individuals; that is, they are in the same room, but not 'one' as Scripture and the tradition would generally describe church. Transmission, in this way, seemed highly reflective of its postmodern context. One wonders if the ontological understanding of oneself as part of the body of Christ is counter-cultural – and the antidote to the loneliness and destructiveness of the highly individualized and autonomous society in which we live, as implied in Bowie Snodgrass's comment that postmodern people are 'ships lost at sea'. We are not sure if Transmission would have made use of this concept of community and oneness in its focus on the individual spiritual journey.

Blesséd, very different from Transmission with full catholic sacramental liturgy, multi-layered worship with an emphasis on the visual, also made full use of rituals. Among them was the taking and replacing of a stone. In the penitential rite, we were invited to take a stone from a 'cairn' in the middle of the liturgical space.

Simon Rundell, presiding at the Eucharist, said to us as we held the stones in our hands:

> Cradle it, and let its hard exterior take on the hardness of your heart. Your stone carries the marks of wind and water, of weather, of spade and drill. It has history. It has past: just like your life. You carry the scars of your experience, maybe outside, maybe within. You hold in your hand something of which there is not another anywhere in the world. Just like you. In places where God is rarely heard, in the dark and dismal places, these stones are ready to cry out in praise to God. Shed onto the stone your hurt, your doubt, your fear, your insecurity, your reluctance to reach out to the God who reaches out to you.

After words of penitence, we rebuilt the cairn as 'a sign of the new Jerusalem'.

Next day at Moot, once again a stone cairn was part of the liturgy, this time in one of the stations. Here we were invited to take a stone and to help build a cairn as a way of expressing a willingness to walk with Jesus in the desert. We were conscious that only 24 hours before, the invitation had been to hold a stone as a sign of the hardness of the heart and to use it to make a cairn, not to symbolize a willingness to walk with Jesus in the desert, but to want to build the new Jerusalem. This was a reminder that emergent churches are using symbol and action in a number of different ways. There are the liturgical symbols and actions that the church recognizes as having some objective meaning (the water of Baptism, for instance, or the bread of the Eucharist). There are the symbols and actions that a community decides to use and to which it gives clear meaning, as with the stones at Blesséd and at Moot. There are the symbols where no meaning is indicated; each participant finding the meaning for themselves, as at Transmission, where 'something happens'. There is misunderstanding and confusion when those who devise liturgy and those who par-ticipate in it are unclear about this.

We found two very different attitudes to congregational movement and gesture. Some communities had clearly not engaged with this or had thought it unimportant. For others it had become a key part of the experience. Given the interest in pilgrimage within the emergent churches, it was surprising that we did not see much in the way of processional movements, but this was probably because the spaces in which most of these communities meet do not allow for it. Magnificent exceptions were Transcendence in York Minster, where we all followed the Book of the Gospels in procession from the Chapter House into the Nave, and St Gregory of Nyssa, where the liturgy moved between two 'rooms' of the church and the movement between one and the other was a processional dance.

One of the deepest experiences we had of communion was at The Crossing in Boston. When Stephanie Spellers improvised the Eucharistic Prayer, there were no words spoken by the community gathered in a circle around the altar; instead we were engaged by gesture, every-one with arms uplifted throughout, apart from during the prayer for the Holy Spirit to work upon the gifts, when everyone extended their hands towards the bread and the wine. The silent participation by gesture touched us deeply. At Moot two weeks later the community gathered around the altar in the same way, and everyone hummed (it was a hum, rather than a drone) through the Eucharistic Prayer while Ian Mobsby sang the words. That had something of the same effect and was followed by the Lord's Prayer in which all stood with hands held out in prayer.

But it was at St Paul's Seattle that we experienced most fully the power of shared gesture for building up a sense of the body of Christ and of a community intent on God. When the liturgy began, the entire congregation stood and turned towards the west where the procession (thurifer, crucifer, acolytes and clergy) stood ready to enter. There was a sense of gathering and meeting. When the entrance began, this procession moved through the church, the community turning as it passed them and everyone bowing to the cross as it passed. Before the last verse of the hymn there was an organ interlude; then, as the last verse began, the ministers, now in front of the altar, bowed to the congregation and the congregation bowed back to them.

Later, the Peace was given and exchanged, conventionally, gently and warmly. The Offertory Hymn was sung. At the end of this there was a procession of gifts by members of the congregation, carrying real bread and the wine poured into a glass chalice so that it could be seen. The elements were censed simply, slowly and unfussily and the three ministers moved slowly around the altar as the presider honoured the gifts with incense. The thurifer then censed the entire community in the same manner. In the Eucharistic Prayer there were slow genuflections and elevations at the words of institution, in which the congregation shared. All bowed at the elevations and crossed themselves at the prayer for sanctification. The Lord's Prayer was sung, with many of the congregation with hands raised. The bread was broken, the Agnus Dei sung and the invitation given. The Distribution was slow and intentional. All in their places remained standing until it was their time to go up to receive, giving a sense of the prayerful recognition of the presence of the body in the gathered community.

At the end of the liturgy, in the final hymn, again there was an organ interlude before the final verse, at which point the ministers bowed to the congregation and the congregation to the ministers. The procession then moved west to the door, the congregation turning as this happened. The presider sang the Dismissal and all responded. People immediately began to move; there were warm greetings from individuals and good congregational care.

What was special about this worship? It was well-ordered Anglican liturgy of a familiar kind, entirely conventional in its shape and text. Three related elements contributed to its being a stunning and moving experience.

First, and most important, there was a deep spirit of engagement by the entire congregation. They did indeed 'carry you in worship', as their service sheet said, by their prayerfulness and attentiveness. The shared spirituality was almost tangible.

The second element was 'performance' and as part of it, very significantly, 'pace'. Clearly everything had been carefully choreographed and rehearsed, yet it did not feel precious or stilted; the whole liturgy was a beautiful 'dance' in which the performers were entirely caught up. The pace at every point was right, never hurried, just a little slower than in most churches, but always moving the shared experience forward.

The third element was the non-verbal participation by the entire community – the turning west at the beginning and the end, the reverencing of the cross at the entry, the mutual bowing between ministers and congregation – creating a sense of a community engaged in something entirely corporate and significant for them.

The appeal of this worship to Generation X and younger includes the high quality of worship leadership, which certainly would have met the expectations of their 'performance culture'. Furthermore, the vehicle of the liturgy gently and pointedly conveyed the offering of what might traditionally be termed mystical spirituality, apparently desired by many in their 20s and 30s.

But this world of gesture is not widespread across the emergent churches and is certainly less pronounced in England than in America. Emergent church leaders to whom we spoke about it found the conversation fascinating and wondered whether this was an area they should explore further.

To turn to the visual, we were surprised to find much less use of video clips, projected images and screens. Quite a few communities, where texts were needed, printed them on simple service sheets. Ethos @ St Nick's, Transcendence, COTA and Blesséd all made extensive use of projected images, but they were the exception. Slowly changing religious images seemed to serve well an atmosphere of worship and prayerfulness. Rapidly changing images tended to leave us confused and unable to retain what we had seen. There was a sense that maybe a reliance on high-tech visuals was passing.

St Gregory of Nyssa is vibrant with colour and religious imagery and artefact. In the centre of the round gathering and meal space, above the altar, is a great overhead mural around the walls, a 'dancing saints' icon and a dancing Christ at the focal point.

Blesséd had created a rich visual setting for its celebration of Mothering Sunday. Dominant was an altar set up for an eastward-facing celebration (this was not their usual custom), loaded with candles, icons, a small statue of Our Lady of Walsingham and flowers. Immediately behind the altar and at the height of the tabletop was a screen for projection. Because it was a kind of 'reredos' it drew us to the altar, rather than away from it, especially in the eucharistic action, though it was a strange cultural mix with the candles, icons and flowers. The altar, like the liturgy, was busy – and there is a need to reflect on the relationship between busyness and complexity.

These were the exceptions. In general, despite a desire for multi-layered liturgy, most of the communities were restrained in relation to visual foci. That restraint was part of a simplicity of furnishing in the worship spaces. Most gave people an option of sitting on chairs (or even in some cases pews) or on the floor (beanbags provided!). Surprisingly in some places, such as at COTA, the seating was very conventional, in rows. In others there were, within the constraints of the building, arrangements in circles or horseshoes, and in several a desire to gather the congregation around the altar for the Eucharist. But the table or the altar was the only constant; there were not many lecterns, no pulpits, few presider's chairs (though at Thad's a high stool for the presider) and not much evidence of fonts. But at St Gregory of Nyssa, highly significantly, as has been said, what you met as you came in was the altar; only beyond it, indeed outside glass doors, was the baptismal font, expressing the theology of that community that we come to Baptism through our participation in the Eucharist.

Other non-verbal elements that were commonly employed in the liturgy were, of course, candles, icons and prayer beads in the prayer stations, incense and, perhaps most importantly, silence. Absolute silence was rare; silence usually meant a time of silent reflection with music to help create the ambience. But we did encounter absolute silence, for instance at St Gregory's, where after the readings and the preaching it created space in what would otherwise have been a liturgy of relentless activity. Open Space, of course, is mainly a silent activity. The most powerful silences were at St Paul's Seattle and we wondered whether a rubric that was repeated at key points in the service encouraged the community to a deep silence. 'Silence and stillness', the rubric said, and there was just that – a total physical stillness and the sense of a spiritual stillness to equal it. It was matched only by the amazing silence and stillness of 500 or so young people in St Mark's Cathedral later that evening (see page 58).

'The Table' at Safe Space included time walking a labyrinth, an activity other emergent churches sometimes also do. It was a model of good practice in a small space, for we managed to walk this labyrinth in a medium-sized living room.

On the living-room floor a simple small labyrinth had been marked out on the carpet with masking tape, with votive lights along the route. We were invited (with staggered starts) to walk the labyrinth; at the beginning and end, and at a number of points on the way, we were to pick up and say, aloud but quietly, the verses of St Patrick's Breastplate that we found on pieces of paper held down by stones, most of them beginning 'I arise today'. At any given point there were three or four of us walking this labyrinth, quite close to one another, having to be sensitive physically and orally to one another.

Until each person's time came to walk the labyrinth we remained silently at the dining table. After walking the labyrinth we returned to the table, where some sat in silence and others spontaneously explored a passage of Scripture. When all had returned we said the last verse of St Patrick's Breastplate together: 'We arise today . . .' At this point one of the group spontaneously suggested that we should indeed arise, stand up, and say the words again standing, which we did. That marked the end of the liturgical element of the evening. The walking of the labyrinth took time, but it was time well spent, time for God and time for the soul. It felt like a way of doing a pilgrimage, all within 25 square metres.

And what of the non-verbal in the Eucharist, alongside the embracing at the Peace and the taking, blessing, breaking and sharing? Already we have mentioned the gathering around the altar, the shared gestures, the glass chalice, the slow and intentional distribution. There was also the involvement of children, never on the edge, always as communicants, at St Gregory's immediately around the altar in front of all the adults, and sharing in the distribution. And, at the Church of the Apostles, warm bread.

Somehow the ash for making soap with which this chapter began and the warm bread with which it ends sum up important elements of the worship of the emergent churches. At one level, ritual is being given a new meaning or, more precisely, it is being used in an open-ended way where people may simply search for the meaning for them. At another level the ancient sacramental signs and symbols of the church, which had for many grown dry and cold, are being taken and renewed, celebrated with more confidence, energy and, yes, warmth. Somehow warm bread seemed to allow the sacrament to be as fresh as the bread with which it was celebrated.

Worshipping communities 5: The Church of the Apostles

Seattle – 28 February 2010

The Church of the Apostles (COTA), in the Fremont neighbourhood of Seattle, came into existence in 2003 as a joint Lutheran/Episcopal initiative, led by the Revd Karen Ward, then a Lutheran pastor, now an Episcopal priest. Beginning across the road from its present church in a church-run café called Living Room, it moved into the former Lutheran Church. They chose the name the Church of the Apostles partly because the embryo community had spent months exploring the Acts of the Apostles. In addition they established a quasi-monastic community and named the church building Fremont Abbey.

COTA has a significance well beyond its neighbourhood. Emerging churches/fresh expressions look to it as a source of inspiration, not least for its music. Karen Ward, who styles herself 'Abbess' of the community, is regarded by many as the 'high priest' of the emerging movement. There is a steady stream of visitors to COTA looking to learn from what has been developed there.

Fremont Abbey is a substantial building, the 'great hall' acting as the liturgical space, with an informal meeting space (the Living Room) near the entrance, an upstairs chapel with icons and candles and chairs set up for the daily office, and a number of smaller rooms that can be adapted for different purposes (as they were that evening for Open Space). In the great hall the furnishings were arranged traditionally, chairs in rows, the altar at the front, the cross, veiled for Lent, behind it. Above the altar was a large screen; to the right of the altar as we faced it were the musicians – violin, drums, two guitars, two vocalists.

We attended the liturgy on Sunday 28 February. The congregation on this Sunday was about 80, mainly in their 20s and 30s, with a few older people.

The liturgy began with 'Opening Words', a scene setting with a recorded male voice and a video of travel – roads, subways – to illustrate the 'Faithful Wanderers' theme. A young woman (Sybil) moved to the microphone to lead the Invocation. We sang a song, 'To You', about God's mercy. The drone through the service was a mysterious music of unknowing. At the beginning of this song the violin was dissonant, a bit flat, perhaps intentionally, conveying a sense of being lost.

The Lectionary readings followed, one after the other, by recorded voices (a different voice for each reading), with an unexciting visual and a drone background. Psalm 27 followed, with a sung extended antiphon and the text being read by the entire community between the repeated antiphon. This led into Open Space (described in Chapter 5).

Brought back together again, after a confession Karen, the presider, stood at the front for the first time to introduce the Peace, which was shared in a traditional way, some embracing, some shaking hands. Karen introduced the offering: 'This is where we take your money,' which provoked laughter! We sang the Offertory Song, 'Lord Jesus, Sun of righteousness', while plates were passed. At the end of the song the money and the bread and wine were brought to the altar. The Eucharistic Prayer was a modified version of Prayer A from the Book of Common Prayer of The Episcopal Church, with a long Intercession interpolated and a drone throughout. The bread was broken in silence, the Lord's Prayer sung and the invitation given. Communion was distributed in front of the altar. The bread was broken by Karen as each person approached her. No paten was used. The bread was warm. There was a Distribution Song, 'Strong weakness'.

What others might call the 'Notices' were now given, but described as 'Invitation into Community'. We said a closing prayer. Karen gave the Blessing: 'The benediction of our faithful God, Father, Son and Holy Spirit', making the sign of the cross with a small wooden cross. We sang the final song, 'How can I keep from singing?' which built to a climax, in some ways the high point of the liturgy. One wanted there to be more verses and the crescendo to continue. The words of the 'Sending' were, as has been said, 'Go, in peace. Wander faithfully.'

This was well-planned and well-ordered liturgy, with an impression of spontaneity at points, but in reality a very tight script. It lasted a little more than an hour, had good variety of pace and, more than most services, developed in terms of mood from being reflective and almost a spectator to celebratory and participatory.

At the beginning the singing by the congregation was very restrained; by the end it was much more engaged, partly no doubt because of the musical choices, but also in response to the dynamic of the liturgy.

In the first part of the liturgy there was little oral participation by the community (listening to a long introduction, an invocation prayer and three readings). Open Space marked a transition into a more engaged mode, and with the Eucharist there came a building sense of involvement. There was also a sense of development within sections of the service; the Affirmation/Confession, for instance, moving from darkness to light.

In terms of conventional eucharistic liturgy the omissions, consistent with some other emerging churches, were creed, absolution and dialogue at the beginning of the Eucharistic Prayer. But this was nevertheless a liturgy very much in line with the conventional shape of eucharistic liturgy, but with less conformity and more creativity in terms of text than in some emergent churches.

We found ourselves pondering this question: around what does community gather and form for this postmodern generation? As Karen Ward noted, and as seemed apparent in other emerging contexts, the Eucharist is central and there is no need to agree on the theology or the practice of it – just to be joined together by it seems to be sufficient. Denominational concerns, loyalty and dedication are low, but devotion to God, Jesus, Scripture and the Eucharist are high.

10

Tune my heart to sing thy grace

———•◆•———

> Come thou Font of every blessing,
> Tune my heart to sing thy grace!
> Streams of mercy never ceasing,
> Call for songs of loudest praise.
> Teach me some melodious sonnet,
> Sung by flaming tongues above.
> Praise the mount! Oh, fix me on it,
> Mount of God's unchanging love.

This eighteenth-century hymn, with words by Robert Robinson, was set to fast-paced rhythmic drums and sung without other accompanying instruments at The Crossing in Boston. It may be heard on their worship CD (see The Crossing's website, <www.crossingboston. org>).

> Of the Father's love begotten,
> Ere the worlds began to be
> He is Alpha and Omega,
> He the source, the ending he,
> Of the things that are, that have been,
> And that the future years shall see,
> Evermore and evermore!

This hymn, traditionally sung at Christmas, with words written by Marcus Aurelius Clemens Prudentius in the fourth century, set to music in the twelfth century, was sung at the Church of the Beloved, a Lutheran church plant in Edmonds, Washington, born from the Church of the Apostles in 2008. 'Of the Father's love begotten' was set to 'an alt country vibe' that had a 'plainchant feel but with a chunky guitar sound'. Tara Ward, a musician for the Church of the Beloved and affiliated to the Church of the Apostles, indicated, 'Sometimes we take old hymns and update them in some new way.

I like to think of it as giving language to the icons of our faith. We like to reclaim the power of what is old for now.'

As we all know, music can move the soul in a way that speech cannot. It engages a different part of the brain from analytical thought and can produce an opening of the mind and the heart that allows for greater engagement of the spirit. While not pretending to be experts in the science of the effect of music, it is obvious that throughout all time and all cultures, music is a key conveyer of life itself. It can raise us to praise and joy, prompt sadness and tears, create anticipation, fear, humour, lightness and darkness. And that is before you add words. Words and music together can do all this and guide our minds theologically and spiritually: reaching new insights, helping us experience deeper love, intimacy, justice, repentance, grace, compassion, clarity, opening our hearts to the worship of God.

Whether the words were from centuries ago or written specifically for the liturgical context of one worship service or a season, we found that music in emergent churches was never boring, was varied in complexity across communities, reflected the importance of the spiritual life and personal transformation, and was understood as an important mode of communication within the worshipping congregation. We encountered much talent and creativity, sometimes expressed with an abundance of musical resources, at other times expressed simply and with just the voices of the congregation. This, of course, is not exclusive to the emergence movement. Traditional church will also understand and value the importance of music, and may have access to fine musical resources, or on the contrary may work only with the gifts and talents already within the congregation.

As with liturgy, music in emergent churches was indigenous to the congregation. We encountered a lot of variety between congregations and within them. But including musicians in the liturgical planning of worship was a consistent factor in emerging congregations, modelling shared authority across areas of artistic expression. At the Church of the Apostles and the Church of the Beloved, both congregations where artistic expression is encouraged in all their members, teams of musicians create liturgical settings and original songs, much of which could be used in congregational singing. Music leaders routinely invite anyone who wants to participate to join the planning for themes or special services, even encouraging members to write songs and prayers. Such openness has produced effective liturgical and musical themes that have included Easter worship in 'blue grass' style (which is a sub-genre of American country music), an African drum circle during the season of Epiphany meant to reflect the calling of the Gentiles through this age-old mode of gathering, and, more generally, original music that is quite literally in conversation with the spiritual journey of the congregation. Ryan March of the Church of the Beloved indicated:

> We are formed in the process of creating liturgy. Meditating on the Scriptures together and asking a few questions always gets us where God wants us to go. In what ways is this [scriptural text] really true? In what ways do we see this in our lives? How we can now bring this into liturgy? This is the process and it is really powerful for us.

Similarly, at Thad's in Los Angeles an inclusive policy is maintained that dictates that anyone who wants to be part of the musical effort is welcome. This means that the trumpet player who hasn't picked up his horn since high school could play with Thad's team. Some of the Church Keys, who are members of the congregation, are also professional musicians. The Church Keys form a spiritually connected small group, which they describe as integral to the formation of Thad's community and its theology. Thad's musician George Daisa spoke of fellow musician Ian Jack, a Thad's song-writer:

> Ian's voice is a prophetic witness to how the Spirit is moving. Interpretation of what Jimmy is teaching sometimes comes through others, like Ian, and then something just 'pops' in the conversation because of what Ian says – he is a witness to the teaching. So, we have expressed what is happening in the community in 'real time'; the music comes right away. Something will happen on Sunday, and on Tuesday there is a song. Ian might labour all night, and then we rehearse it and put it out there as part of the conversation.

Ian commented:

> Writing the music engages the key concepts coming right out of the community discussion. Then, the music brings out people's feelings and thoughts about God and opens up the community for more conversation. Music is the way we relay it back to the body and that way of reflecting feels right. It is very intuitive. The writing is like prayer, which is being opened up and is rattling around with God. Sometimes it's clear and sometimes not, although we are always trying to support

the biblical message. The interpretation of the Spirit at work in the community is what is really happening – and to give it voice is for the glory of God. To me that is worship.

At Thad's, music is nearly all original and not necessarily repeated. It is a part of the theological development and 'feedback loop' with the 'teaching', based on the week's Scripture reading that is largely done by Jimmy Bartz. Thad's exemplifies what we found in a number of churches; that is, the process of the development of liturgy and music is itself worshipful. Song-writers are greatly edified and inspired as they are part of the formation of Christian community and the development of the spiritual lives of worshippers. They are not performing, but completely integrated in every way with the worshipping community.

For example Hunter Perrin, a member of Thad's and a professional musician (guitarist for the John Fogerty Band), writes music and leads worship for the congregation. He is an important listener, giving voice to what is spiritually happening in the congregation. In a song called '40 days', he noted the use of minor and major chords to help convey that, while life might feel confusing and unsure, God is always there. He says:

> I wrote it for Lent. I wanted to offer to people an experience where they could feel as they listened through the wilderness experience of Jesus, a kind of murky time, which I wrote in a minor key; and then putting the chorus in a major key while singing about God's constant presence. Like, it's okay even if life feels like it isn't. People told me that they kept singing the refrain all week and it helped them know God was around.

Perrin noted too that he tries not to be too precise in his writing, so that people will seek out the scriptural text and discover what it means for themselves. As he says, 'The lyrics should prompt questions instead of answering them. I'm not here to give my answer, but to help others find their answer.'

40 days

> 40 days and 40 nights I was hungry
> asked me could I make bread from the stone
> if I am who I say I am
> I could do it on my own I could do it on my own

Chorus
and as he filled me up with pride softly singing through his song
I was glad you're by my side
and you've been there all along and you've been there all along

for 40 days I looked out at the kingdom
he said that he would give it to me
if I am who I say I am
I would always be free I would always be free

Chorus

for 40 nights I was placed on the temple
asked me would I jump down to the ground
if I am who I say I am
I would not get turned around I would not get turned around

Chorus

While Thad's was unique among the congregations we visited in that it produced so much original music for its own worship, it is a strong example of the communal theological process that creates music for contextual worship. Even congregations that limit the creation of music to a designated group still function with this same level of dynamic and integrative process, always including the theological conversation occurring in the congregation. There seemed a lack of 'politicking', if you will, around music; in the case of familiar or expected hymns the fact that they have been sung for years was not a reason for their inclusion in a particular worship setting, as one might find in a traditional church.

The evolution of music in emergence (that is, inclusive of both emerging and emergent) congregations in the United Kingdom is worth noting, since this is an area of mutual impact with the American context. Given our Anglican kinship, it made sense to us that American emergent leaders would have been influenced by this progression, especially since other contemporary forms of music (used more in inherited churches, it seemed, than in the emergent churches we experienced) are most prominently connected with so-called non-denominational churches or the Roman Catholic renewal movement. Sue Wallace of Visions and Transcendence reflected to us that the music of emergence churches in the UK has been musically influenced in some way by the Nine o'clock Service (NOS), started in 1986 in St Thomas Crookes Church in Sheffield. While most people would not know that the seeds of musical change were cast in that context, it was of significant impact because of its high standard, run by a full-time band, supported through sacrificial giving and community living.

Sue noted this further progression:

> In the first two years of NOS's existence this music was Goth and Alternative (hence the term 'alternative worship'), but in 1988 House music hit the clubs in Sheffield. The musicians realized that this style of music was an appropriate and powerful vehicle for worship and so the group wrote songs that went with this idiom, mixing home-grown tunes written in their church studio with DJ'd backing tracks. Songs were written over tracks such as 'Passion' by Gat Decor, instrumental dance tunes which could be used as a basis for home-grown melodies. Meanwhile prayers were spoken over the more ambient dance tracks around at the time. Albums by the Orb, Leftfield, Sven Vath and Moby were all used instead of organ voluntaries or as backing for the spoken liturgy.

Other influences included the Late, Late Service of Glasgow, which in addition to other influences theologically and musically incorporated the Iona Community, with its offering of Celtic spirituality. Indeed the Celtic influence has been quite strong among the emergent churches in Britain, as has the music of the Taizé community, which has in some places produced an emphasis on simple song and chant. Sue Wallace also noted that these days, 'it almost feels like anything goes musically in some alternative worship services,' but she added, 'I think that really the unspoken rule is anything goes as long as it isn't "*that*".' 'That' in this context means the Hillsongs, Spring Harvest and Vineyard evangelical repertoire. There is some reticence to use songs that are perceived as being overly romantic in their devotion to Christ (sometimes known as 'Jesus is my boyfriend' music). Wallace says that there is also a positive drift towards the use of songs that have ancient and deep roots, which come from an ancient Christian tradition, such as that provided by the Celtic and Orthodox churches.

In speaking with Ian Mobsby of Moot in London, we heard about this process of sorting through how music and liturgy could work together for that specific context. Mobsby explained that music was in transition at Moot in part due to the dominance of contemporary evangelical Christian music. He indicated that the more exclusive theological message had been a deterrent in the discovery of Moot's own musical style and message. They tended to use simple chants, such as those from Taizé, and to create chants for the liturgy as a way of employing music in worship. His hope was that they would progress towards greater development of a music team that could exercise an indigenous creativity appropriate to their 'spiritual seeker' population.

This indigenous means of creating and providing music in the emerging setting communicates a basic reality of church music. No matter what its style, it conveys theology. The churches we visited were inclusive in all sorts of ways: gender, sexual orientation, age, and cultural, personal and religious experience. While there may have been some variation in emphasis in each congregation, prevailing were themes of God's abiding love, presence, forgiveness and accessibility as it is seen in Jesus. Whether music was original, traditional hymnody, chant, jazz or blues, texts and tone tended to convey the message of a loving and attentive God worthy of a relationship that had the power to transform one's life.

Theology, context and process impact detail. Specifically we witnessed subtle but effective use of music in a number of ways. For instance, setting the mood for worship was often accomplished with music rather than with verbal instruction. We heard all varieties of music – instrumental playing, upbeat music and singing or gentle chant – before worship to cue people towards a focus on God and to direct their attention towards a communal experience. At the Church of the Apostles effective use of a slow-tempo, slightly disharmonic minor sound was used to begin this Lenten worship with its theme of 'Faithful Wandering': for the congregation the dissonance of the music included the possibility of feeling lost or disoriented in the journey. While church is perceived by those outside of it as a place where people project an image of having happy, well-organized lives, music was effectively used to convey that this may or may not be so. This level of honesty is encouraged in emerging churches and the music can underscore the inclusive message of acceptance of a person's spiritual journey just as it may be, even if it is confused or painful. Pastorally, as noted, such songs can be a sort of spiritual companionship during the week, between worship services. But Christianity is a faith of hope, and in this same service music was also used to contrast, or perhaps even challenge, loneliness or confusion as normative (as some might think it is) with upbeat joy and confidence. At the conclusion of this same worship service with its faithful wandering theme we were sent out into the world singing the popular song, 'How can I keep from singing?', a very upbeat and joyful piece of music that the congregation sang confidently and well.

As with traditional Anglican worship, music was used in the liturgy itself. We encountered use of the psalms frequently, in traditional translations and chant patterns or contemporary phrasing and settings, as was the case at Transmission. Isaac Everett's *Emergent Psalter* provides Isaac's own translation of the text and musical chant for this 'icon of faith'. At Moot the Affirmation of Faith was said with a drum accompaniment, offering a rap expression. Spoken prayers included a sung refrain, such as a Kyrie or other simple phrase. During the Eucharistic Prayer we heard in a number of settings use of a drone – a single note held by the congregation, providing a gentle hum that supported the spoken liturgy very effectively. At Moot, when the liturgy was sung, responses were begun on the sustained note, giving clear non-verbal instruction of what the starting pitch was. Not only was this beautiful use of a simple musical tone and singing, it was an effective way to engage people in liturgy that is often spoken by the congregation or the president alone.

We also encountered beautiful chanting of the Gospel. In recent years liturgical trends have stressed that the Gospel should be read, but we encountered several occasions where it was chanted, traditionally or with stylized settings for the particular text, with great beauty and effectiveness. Our experience was that the musical setting prompted enhanced ability to remember the story, with personal reflection on the Scriptures lasting well beyond the worship event.

In all, the liturgical aspect of music in worship accomplished several things. First, it contributed to the aesthetic beauty of worship, especially since gifted musicians and leaders offered quality singing, chanting, instrumental playing and musicianship. As well, emergent churches create worship thematically or at least with sensitivity to the season. Music is understood and intended as a significant aspect of the transformation that is on offer in emergent worship. As music tends to open both the left and right sides of the brain, it can increase one's ability to take in the theme or focus of the season, intellectually and spiritually, naturally enhancing the intensity of the worship experience and creating a lasting impression through which one's prayerful reflection might continue.

While this chapter has used illustrations from emergent congregations that have sophisticated and accomplished musical resources, most of the churches we visited did not. Just five of the emergent congregations visited used recorded music (interestingly these were all in England), one used two guitars to lead congregational singing, and one had a single drum. This is undoubtedly related to the expense of professional musicians, but also to the reality that congregational singing is a somewhat counter-cultural activity in this day and age. More and more, we are a listening culture when it comes to music. The traditional pattern of hymn singing that assumes the ability to read music is no longer a common cultural skill. Just as with the Christian story itself, worship leaders must not assume previous knowledge of what traditional church members may already find familiar. Hymns or even tunes may be completely new to those who have not been part of a worshipping congregation previously.

Nevertheless, congregational singing builds up the communal experience of the worshipping body, contributing to a sense of oneness and spiritual unity. Donald Schell, former co-rector of St Gregory of Nyssa, now facilitating workshops and leadership courses in music and liturgy with All Saints' Company (<www.allsaintscompany.org>), believes music to be an essential spiritual practice. Liturgical singing, which can be simple and accessible, facilitates easy movement through liturgy for those new to the church experience. This may lead to greater participation over time than recitation of words. As well, the opportunity to repeat words and tunes over weeks allows reflection on Christian doctrine and theology, particularly that of the Eucharist, so central to the Anglican experience. St Gregory of Nyssa, while not an emergent church, uses no instrumentation, but a choir leads the congregational singing as well as offering anthems, and worship leaders with beautiful singing voices lead the liturgy. St Gregory's strongly emphasizes the use of paperless music (now produced by the All Saints' Company). These are simple, often one-line chants that a worship leader may encourage the congregation to start joining in with – they are easily repeatable phrases that require no ability to read music or previous group singing experience. Harmonies may be added by those capable, but are not required. The theological concept is often simple: 'Lord have mercy', 'Open my heart', 'Alleluia', 'Jesus is with us, let us bless the Lord.' Such memorable chants may provide opportunities for prayer and meditation, allowing Scripture, the language of faith and a personal experience of God to sink into one's soul in a way that may not happen with traditional hymnody or even contemporary music. Of course, when one considers music throughout the ages, unaccompanied congregational singing of simple chants or verses is dominant. It is only in recent years that the use of bands or diverse stylistic offerings has seemed the norm.

In those congregations that used more sophisticated musical resources, such as Thad's or the Church of the Apostles, we witnessed the use of good-quality sound equipment and sometimes video systems. Although used creatively in enhancing ways, this was not normative. In fact we noted that many communities were going 'low-tech', using closer seating configurations, a greater variety of voices, and chant in the liturgy in order to maintain audibility.

As noted previously in this book, emergents value quality and beauty in worship, the latter more subjective than the first in this high-tech culture. Culturally this generation is accustomed to high quality in the performance of liturgy and music because they live in a world that is technologically fast, accurate and well executed. There is little room in their universe for anything poorly performed. Emergents spend considerable amounts of time in preparation and rehearsal, reflection and improvement on matters of audibility, creative expression, accessibility to the worship experience, and of course the message they are communicating. While in traditional churches regularly used patterns of worship are of value in and of themselves, the motivation for the process of reflection and change in emerging worship is to provide a more accessible, inclusive and edifying experience for the congregation. They will let go of material that is no longer useful in effective communication of the good news of the gospel and in spiritual transformation. Ultimately, this process of musical and liturgical preparation and delivery provides a rich spiritual and ecclesial life for worship leaders that in turn provides spiritual food for the congregation and all those who might move in and out of their common life. Whether a congregation chooses less sophisticated or more complex music, requiring many musicians and instruments or none, such constant engagement with the spiritual journey of the worshippers, the gospel story, and the gifts of the Christian tradition provide a rich context for God's active presence in the life of the community and freedom for the manifestation of the Spirit in worship. In the end, the process and the product are equally important and powerful conveyers of the message of the Christian faith.

Words for worship 5: Beginning and ending

Prayer of invocation

Father,
None of this is clear.
Life isn't clear.
Relationships aren't clear.
Paths aren't clear.
Callings aren't clear.
And sometimes it even feels like you aren't even clear.
So come in and sit and wrestle with us as we gather
    today among this community of grace and truth and
    love.
As we seek to get a better understanding of all of this
    and how we do this thing called life.
As we come to you with all of our doubts and fears; all
    of our anxieties; all of our plans; and all of our lack of
    clarity.
Father, we ask that in and thru all of that, you remind us,
    once again, of those promises that you have made to
    us that ARE clear.
Brilliantly clear . . .
just hard to believe.
So as we wander and have wandered; help us to wander
    in faith that you are a God who fulfils your promises –
even when, to us, they seem laughably absurd at times.
Help us to listen to and trust in your still and small voice
    that always mysteriously leads us home.

Closing prayer

'Faithful' and 'wanderer',
seeming opposites, yet one drives the other.
There's no true faith without wandering.
There's no true wandering without faith.
Holy God, be faithful to your promises.
Lead us and guide us to home.

Church of the Apostles, Seattle

11

Living the wonderful and sacred mystery

———◆———

Both The Episcopal Church's Book of Common Prayer and the Church of England's *Common Worship: Daily Prayer* include (in two slightly different translations) an eighth-century prayer from the Gelasian Sacramentary.

> God of unchangeable power and eternal light, look favourably on your whole Church, that wonderful and sacred mystery and by the tranquil operation of your perpetual providence carry out the work of our salvation: and let the whole world feel and see that things which were cast down are being raised up and things which had grown old are being made new and that all things are returning to perfection through him from whom they took their origin, even Jesus Christ our Lord. (*Common Worship: Daily Prayer*)

The leaders of the emergent churches, with their desire to engage with contemporary culture and their willingness to explore and recover treasures from the past, engage creatively with the aspiration 'that things which were cast down are being raised up and things which had grown old are being made new'. We experienced strong links to the Anglican liturgical tradition and mission culture, as well as identification with the ethos and theology of the liberal and inclusive strand of Anglicanism. That is not to say that we found emergents unorthodox in their Trinitarian theology or their Christology (quite the contrary), but sociologically liberal and inclusive of all sorts and conditions of people, reflecting their place in the inherited Anglican tradition. This seemed to us consistent and clear among the emergent churches we experienced, even though the contextual expression varied between England and the United States. We now explore how this gift of the inherited church continues to develop through liturgy in emergent churches.

But whether in England or the United States, the question we have asked ourselves is whether the emergent churches have firm hold of the concept of the one holy catholic and apostolic Church and of the communion of saints. The answer, clearly, is that in some respects they have, but there is also sufficient emphasis on the local and the provisional that they may sometimes fail to buy in to the bigger picture. In this chapter we will look at the ways in which, with their mission-focused and inclusive emphasis, they do indeed live within the Church as a 'wonderful and sacred mystery', as the prayer describes it, and the extent to which they might discover new depths to that belonging.

Interestingly the gifts and challenges of the inherited church to the emergent churches in both England and the United States are consistent with one another. We have described some striking similarities and they emerge from the same strand within Anglicanism, but the reasons for their being are not the same. In England some of the fresh expressions, including several that we visited, were to some extent at least shaped and formed in reaction to conservative evangelical theology, some of it within the Church of England, and were seeking to be inclusive of those whom others might leave out. These include gay and lesbian people, those unable to accept some conservative teaching about faith and ethics and those in the midst of uncertainty about their faith lives. But that was not mirrored in the United States, where The Episcopal Church does not have as strong a conservative and evangelical wing as the Church of England, and where many traditional congregations embrace a wider diversity of people. Emergent congregations in the United States tend to attract younger people primarily, who would be sociologically liberal, but are able to gather in one congregation expressing a variety of theological approaches.

There was also a missional difference between the two countries in terms of the kind of communities the emergent churches were trying to serve. In both countries congregations are planted in order to reach those the church otherwise may not because traditional congregations are unable to 'speak the language' of the postmodern generation. In the American context, that often means forming a community embedded in its neighbourhood in a way that other Episcopal churches, usually gathered churches, have not tended to be. In England, where church life continues to be community based, the fresh expressions movement often works through non-geographical networks, in some cases without a strong sense of solidarity with the local. This is increasingly true with online communication facilitating all sorts of new paradigms of community building. This process of creating new congregations, either as an outreach of an existing church or as a new plant, is consistent with how congregations have been established in the Anglican tradition, especially in recent times; that is, relative to the cultural context in which they will exist, even if geography is not the primary motive. While the essence of Anglican Christianity has been expressed in the establishment of many churches, the 'local' cultural context has always been taken into consideration. All in all, the motivation, from one country to another and one emergent church to another, may vary significantly but the theology and the worship may be remarkably similar.

As noted throughout this book, on both sides of the Atlantic we experienced the creative liturgical expression that emergent leaders share from the fullness of the Christian tradition. They are not reinventing the faith but re-energizing it and sharing it in their postmodern context. They receive the tradition graciously and are very good stewards of it. The idea that the essence of the Christian faith or the beauty of our liturgy will be lost if we do not keep things the way they are was not borne out in our observation. Quite the opposite: we experienced well-informed, interesting, innovative, beautiful, thoughtful and tradition-based worship that connected effectively with the spirituality and life-experience of the local context that the leaders wanted to reach.

In emergent congregations our Anglican liturgical and missional heritage is an important part of identity. As noted, they have taken their lead from a particular strand of our church. How liturgy takes shape flows from theological emphasis. For example, when one enters a church one can see what the theology is likely to be by the placement of the altar, the font, the pulpit, the seating. When one experiences the words of the liturgy it becomes even clearer what that emphasis is and what sort of Anglicanism is being expressed.

Liturgy in these churches reflects the fact that they see themselves as being part of their environment, rather than expecting the world they are seeking to reach to conform to an inherited expression of church. Especially as part of the postmodern world, emergent leaders understand themselves to be in a partnership, with the traditional church and the people with whom they live 'locally'. The emergent leaders we met understand themselves as cultural missionaries, so to speak, in constant dialogue with the local community of which they are a part and the Church they love. They have inherited a heart-felt imperative to be in two places at once, drawing on an Anglican tradition that culture is always a relevant part of the mission conversation. It is good to be reminded of Archbishop William Temple's often quoted words: 'The Church is the only institution that exists primarily for the benefit of those who are not its members.' Emergent leaders offer a postmodern expression of this value and they are spiritually at home in this mind-set.

The heart for mission, the heart for reconciliation, the ability to listen and live in the wider culture and convey back to the institution, are central to our Anglican understanding of ministry and mission, whether at home or abroad. Liturgy and mission go hand in hand in our tradition. It is expressed in its most focused way in the Ordinal of both the Church of England and The Episcopal Church in relation to the ministry of the diaconate, which makes an intentional connection between church and world. In the English *Common Worship: Ordination Services*, the deacon is to 'reach into the forgotten corners of the world', though, to be truthful, this distinctive ministry of the deacon is better understood in The Episcopal Church than among Anglicans in England. The role of the deacon in this connection, as in others, is, of course, to model such ministry to the whole Church, to which it belongs. In our own day there is a particular need for all Christians to engage in this two-way conversation of faith and context that has always been a part of Anglicanism.

One of the ways in which emergent churches have learned, and can learn, from the inherited church is in how we approach the work of mission. As culture and theological understandings have shifted, so have liturgy and prayer in relation to mission. There have been over the years significant changes, for example in how we understand those 'out there', people not part of the church, and our relationship with them. An example from the liturgies of our churches during the twentieth century illustrates this.

In 1928 the English Proposed Prayer Book (which never received the approval of Parliament, but was, nevertheless, widely used through the 50 years following), included as a prayer for mission these words:

God of all the nations upon the earth, remember the multitudes of the heathen, who, though created in thine image, are ignorant of thy love; and, according to the propitiation of thy Son Jesus Christ, grant that by the prayers and labours of thy holy Church they may be delivered from all superstition and unbelief and brought to worship thee; through him whom thou hast sent to be our salvation, the Resurrection and Life of all the faithful, the same thy Son Jesus Christ our Lord.

By the time this prayer had appeared in the 1979 Book of Common Prayer of The Episcopal Church, it had been modified to read rather differently:

O God of all the nations of the earth: remember the multitudes who have been created in your image but have not known the redeeming work of our Savior Jesus Christ; and grant that, by the prayers and labors of your holy Church, they may be brought to know and worship you as you have been revealed in your Son; who lives and reigns with you and the Holy Spirit, one God, for ever and ever.

The heathen, superstition, ignorance and unbelief have all disappeared as the church learns to use language differently and, more important, to understand those outside it in a more positive way. Even in its revised form the prayer represents an approach that perhaps belonged to an earlier age than when it appeared in 1979, and perhaps a new prayer in the same book captures more readily the spirit of that age:

Ever living God, whose will it is that all should come to you through your Son Jesus Christ: inspire our witness to him, that all may know the power of his forgiveness and the hope of his resurrection; who lives and reigns with you and the Holy Spirit, one God, now and for ever.

The sequence is complete when the Church of England's *Common Worship* in 2000 abandons all the earlier prayers in favour of one that reads:

Almighty God, who called your Church to witness that you were in Christ reconciling the world to yourself: help us to proclaim the good news of your love, that all who hear it may be drawn to you; through him who was lifted up on the cross, and reigns with you in the unity of the Holy Spirit, one God, now and for ever.

With each new prayer the language changes, for our relationship with the world beyond the church changes also, in response to multiculturalism, in response to a new society where we more easily learn to honour and respect those whose understanding of both life and religion are different from our own and, of course, in response to postmodernism with its more subjective approach to truth. Indeed the emergent churches will perhaps want to move on both the argument and therefore also the liturgical expression of it to reflect a gentler approach to people who have not embraced the Christian gospel. We have moved a long way from talk of unbelief and superstition, though there still exists in some places a mind-set of seeing people beyond the church as outsiders needing to join us. The very word 'unchurched' suggests this attitude and the idea that it is permissible to define people who do not identify with the Christian faith from our vantage point. Instead we need to see them as partners in a conversation of faith, with something to offer of their own experience, even though it varies from our own. Emergent Anglicans, reflecting on that sequence of mission prayers, might want to ask the question, 'Is it God's will that *all* should come to God through Jesus?' and would likely want to leave room for graceful conversation around the exclusivity of Christ. The inherited interplay between faith and culture continues and the emergent context provides a very dynamic setting for this conversation. This will, of course, be a source of anxiety for some Anglicans. This can be a tense conversation in the church, since some will hold passionately to the view that culture should never impact on faith. Faith cannot always bow to culture.

There is also a development within the inherited churches that the emergent churches are ready to pick up, on how we understand this mission. There has been an increased emphasis on the *missio dei*; it is God's mission. The Church's task, as the Archbishop of Canterbury has said, is 'to find out what God is doing and to join in'. To some extent that means speaking more of 'God's mission' than 'the Church's mission', but not if that implies that there is no commitment to playing a part. On the contrary, the emphasis now is on the calling of every Christian to be part of that mission, not to leave the sharing of the good news to professionals, ordained ministers or 'missionaries'. The emergent churches understand that, perhaps more clearly than many in the inherited churches, who somehow imagine the *missio dei* happens without them.

This impetus to mission is perhaps the key issue where the emergent churches are receiving from the inherited church through the ages and investing with new energy. We identified five other areas where they are receiving from the inherited church and can learn from its present-day life as well as its history.

The first relates to the personnel of worship. The shifting under-standing of the work of mission to include both laity and clergy to some extent reflects the pattern of leadership of worship in emergent churches. As we have already noted, worship in their context nor-mally involves a shared leadership. Many will have been involved in the preparation of worship, whether through planning or composing the music or through creating stations for Open Space. When it comes to the time for worship, there will rarely be dominance by one person; nearly always the leadership will be collaborative. This reflects an understanding of the nature of the Church, shared with those in the inherited churches who have recovered the Pauline sense of the Body of Christ, with its limbs and organs, gifts and ministries (1 Corinthians 12; Ephesians 4.1–16). In making this emphasis, we wondered whether some of the emergent churches might see that a gentle presidency of worship could be something that helps worship to flow and to have unity and security. The role of the presider (in The Episcopal Church) or president (in the Church of England) is not, except in relation to the sacraments, necessarily a priestly role, nor is the pre-sider always the leader of the community. It is simply that where a number of people share leadership in worship, each with their par-ticular function and input, it is often helpful for one of them to have a particular role as an 'anchor', drawing the community together and holding the different parts of the liturgy in an overarching unity. The presider, visible and communicating as much by gesture and atten-tiveness than by words, does not need to speak often, and certainly should not dominate; delegates much but draws together. Such a ministry will, in small communities, need to be very low profile. As a community grows larger it can be a significant contribution to the cohesion of the worship. It is something the contemporary liturgical movement in the inherited churches might be able to share with the emergent communities.

A second area where the inherited churches have wisdom to share is what is offered to the Christian in a deep sacramental life lived consciously within the communion of the Church, the 'wonderful and sacred mystery' that unites every century and draws earth and heaven together. We have been left wondering several times about the open-ended offering of Christian teaching we saw in most congregations, and about what long-term impact that will have on those seeking, as well as upon the ecclesiology being formed. There is a lot of room between the traditional sermon of the inherited church – one person teaching their interpretation of Anglican Christianity – and 'Open Space', the 'buffet' offering of spiritual food from which people may pick and choose. The Holy Spirit is understood to guide in both instances, but, again, the intention of the community to form in a particular way may need to be more clearly identified in emergent churches. We did not always experience a strong sense that these congregations recognized they were connected to the wider church around them in this time, nor a strong cosmic sense of being part of the one, holy, catholic and apostolic Church throughout eternity. Some emerging leaders, as well as those in the inherited church, expressed concern about 'spiritual tourism'; that is, people coming in and 'grazing' for the spiritual food they find appealing, but not wrestling with the parts that make them uncomfortable or challenged. This pushes up against historical Christianity, which has always understood Truth as objective and to a greater or lesser degree absolute, and that the Church Universal is a part of something much bigger than its local self. Furthermore, the life-long, ever-deepening commitment of the Christian has always been normative; a process expressed in both Scripture and other writings throughout the ages. People growing, developing and maturing in the faith is inherent in the Christian life. Shall emerging congregations be only for the beginner or those returning to be followers of Jesus, the casual seeker, shopper or grazer; or can they be communities which can include a variety of developmental faith stages as well as the other forms of diversity they are so good at embracing? Is there value in these newer emerging congregations 'growing up', so to speak, better articulating and owning their local ecclesiology as it relates to the universal, the Church of the ages and the communion of saints, perhaps positively impacting sustainability?

The third area relates to seeing the long-term picture. On our journey to emergent congregations we noted a consistent lack of concern from leaders about the sustainability and longevity of this movement and of the congregations they led. If the institutional church is overly concerned with survival, it may be that the emerging church is not concerned enough. There could be a balance to be struck between holding too tightly to an identity and not holding tightly enough. Consistently, when leaders were asked what a particular congregation would be like in five years' time, or where they themselves would be in five years, they said, 'I don't know.' These communities are typically small and the presence of the leader makes an important difference. Should the leader leave, ministry by a single recognized leader, probably ordained, probably paid, might well come to an end. Leaders all expressed the view that this could just be the natural life of that particular ministry. While ministries come and go, it would seem that the clergy leaders of these congregations will need to develop other leaders in the life of the congregation so that even if the priest departs the ministry could be sustained. In other words, might the maturity level of these congregations develop enough as to weather the storms of transition, but not over-correct so much as to become systemically entrenched in a way that would lose the flexibility required of ministry in this postmodern culture? As is the case with all churches, paying attention to its systemic health and its development is a very important task for the emergent congregation.

There is something at stake here: that is, the long-term presence of inclusive churches that are in the midst of postmodern culture. It could be possible to be patient, gentle as well as innovative, about the length of time commitment the Christian life takes, and also recognize in the movement God's longer-term strategy for the sharing and planting (with some permanence) of the good news. In other words, the whole Church needs to claim space for emergent congregations in the Church Universal. On a day-to-day level, this might be accomplished through a more structured offering of the sacramental markers of Baptism and Confirmation that serve to develop commitment. In our experience as bishops, we find these experiences to be deeply moving milestones of a life of grace, drawing people into the big picture of God's saving work, as opposed to ritualistic events that must be done. Many inherited churches manage such integration well, especially when they understand that their survival is not just to keep the doors open for their own sake, but so that people of all types and conditions, over time, can find their way to Christ, having a spiritual home. While emerging churches are 'in the moment' of this postmodern age, it is important to remember that all of creation – culture and church – are an integrated part of God's seemingly lengthy plan of salvation. The Church through the ages has wisely kept the perspective that we are an expression of a greater mystery and that 'moments' are part of God's eternal life of love for all.

A fourth gift of the inherited church to emergent churches is the gift of sacred space. The kingdom is within and travels with a person, as Jesus said, but spiritual space can be an extraordinary gift to the pilgrim. Even though emerging congregations often operate on lean budgets and are hosted by institutional churches, the physical experience of a sanctuary enhances spiritual nurture. Settings such as the very beautiful St Gregory of Nyssa and York Minster or the cosy New York apartment of Transmission offer a physical connection to an internal spiritual reality. Compline at St Mark's Cathedral in Seattle speaks strongly to this reality. It is a service that has been going on for 50 years, helping people journey from the inception of a conscious faith life into a call to the fullness of life – falling in love, solitude, prayer, successes, ordination – holding the great variety of encounters, vocations and experiences of so many people over time. Physical space also offers the witness of faithful Christians who were good stewards of the future, providing a place for seekers to discover God. Buildings speak something of the past, offer nurture to the present, and challenge our stewardship for those who will come after us. This is yet another way ecclesiology is developed in congregations, connecting the church between generations.

Another gift of the inherited church that is always with a person is, of course, the inner life. This is a fifth area where emergent churches may learn from a renewed openness and freshness in the inherited church. Christian spirituality is not, of course, confined to buildings, but primarily resides in the heart and soul. We were pleased with the spiritual disciplines, qualities we saw in some of the churches we visited, and felt this was a good way for the Christian life to be nurtured and deepened. Brian McLaren, in his book *Finding our Way: The Return of the Ancient Practice*, identifies helpfully seven sacred practices. He sees their origin in the life of Abraham and reminds his readers that these practices are to be found in common in the three great Abrahamic religions: Judaism, Islam and Christianity. The seven are pilgrimage, fasting, giving, sacred meal, fixed time common prayer, sabbath and a liturgical year. In general Anglicanism, especially in its more catholic expression, has kept all of these alive through the centuries and in recent years has imbued them with fresh vitality. We saw all seven being taken seriously in emergent churches, though most of them are at a very early stage of development; in relation to all of them the inherited churches have much to offer (as well as a little to receive). Indeed, exploring the more neglected of these spiritual practices – perhaps pilgrimage, fasting and sabbath – is something that inherited and emergent churches would do well to pursue together.

We found on our travels great openness among emergent leaders to be in conversation with the inherited church. There was no resistance that we experienced, and in fact we were warmly welcomed, embraced and received as bishops. The two entities need to be in conversation with one another, otherwise it is a movement of nothing, and the traditional church will be missing its point of contact with a mission field it finds challenging to meet. The Anglican tradition is in so many ways poised to be a place of faith for the postmodern generation precisely because we are a church that is incarnational, relational and conversational. We are a church that at the very least tolerates diversity, and at our best embraces and enjoys it. Emergents are taking this strong, inclusive strand of Anglicanism into the postmodern world, laden with the gifts of the ages – ready to offer them back to the inherited church.

Worshipping communities 6: Moot

London – 14 March 2010

Moot came into existence in 2003. It was founded by Ian Mobsby, then a lay person, now a priest of the Diocese of London. It understands itself as a new monastic community. Although we visited it on a single occasion for worship, Moot is clear that worship (of various kinds) is only a part of its life, which is held together by worship, mission and community.

Moot's particular aim is to be a place for the never churched, rather than the dechurched. Ian understands Moot's ministry more in terms of post-secular than postmodern, appealing to the aesthetic through the multi-sensory. He identifies three kinds of unchurched who have been drawn into Moot. There are those who have been 'new-agers', mostly in their 30s and 40s; those whom he describes as the products of the darker side of materialism, seeking pain relief and health; and the 'complete displacement' people, mainly young men, needing to be active, more interested in spiritual walking than in worship. Moot meets people not at the stage of 'deconstruction', but 'reconstruction'.

The monastic community element of Moot is central to its self-understanding. Ian calls it the bedrock. Its members, with their 'rhythm (rule) of life', renew their commitment before the Bishop of London annually at Easter. The community has its Moot Community Council for governance, and its own electoral roll. There is a weekly midweek meeting for meditation and study. There is a service every Sunday, with the Eucharist monthly. There are in a sense two groupings within the community, one with families, one with younger adults without children. They come together in the community meeting.

Ian Mobsby's background is in occupational health work and as a Southwark ordinand. In 2003, with the Bishop of London's encouragement, he began a monthly alternative worship service at St Matthew's Westminster. He believes that the fact that this happened in a church with a strong catholic tradition has helped to give shape to Moot's life as a contemplative, sacramental and missional community. Ian always wanted the community to be mission focused, even more than worship focused. The bishop backed this, obtained the funding for his post and ordained him as a deacon. He was priested a year later.

In January 2011, Moot finally moved into a permanent home: St Aldermary's, London. Until then, the community met in a number of different churches. It now has hopes for a base for mission, with café, lounge and gallery space, as well as liturgical space. Longer term also there is the hope of a house where community members could live and as a further base for ministry to those reconstructing their lives.

We visited Moot on Sunday 14 March. Members of the community were gathered for the monthly Eucharist at St Mary Woolnoth in the City of London. It was a small group, 20 of us, mainly in their 20s and 30s. We gathered in the chancel seats. There were three stations set up in the nave, and a screen set up to show a film clip; the instrumental accompaniment was a single drum, though there was also recorded music. Before the altar was a version of the hospitality of Abraham icon. But the overall physical setting was very conventional church!

The liturgy began with an Invocation and a Taizé chant, after which a young woman, Helen, introduced the service.

> This evening we stand in a liminal space, in the fourth and last week of Lent. Tonight we celebrate life at the edge, in a search for inner searching. So we come together to worship God, to reflect on our lives as we look towards Holy Week and the story of our Lord's passion. So as we seek to follow God, let us reflect on our own inner need for freedom and peace.

Confession led into 'Readings and Story Telling' and the introduction to the Homily was a 'video reflection' from *The Last Temptation of Christ*. Film as metaphor is important for Moot. The Homily prepared the way for the Stations, lasting 15 minutes; all three reflected a thoughtful, sophisticated and literate community. Coming together again, there was an Affirmation of Faith, the Peace, a second chant and the censing of the altar and the icon.

In the Eucharistic Prayer we were invited to sing and maintain a single note through the first part of the prayer, which we did, singing responses on that note and otherwise maintaining a gentle hum. The hum – it was indeed more of a hum than a drone – seemed to deepen the level of participation. The Lord's Prayer and the Breaking of the Bread followed and we sang the Agnus Dei, repeating each line after Ian, but with the repeated use of the clause 'you take away the selfishness of the world', instead of the traditional 'sin of the world'. The Distribution was conventional, two ministers moving around the circle. Everyone received. We said a Post-Communion Prayer together and were dismissed with a Blessing.

The liturgy was a serious and worshipful Eucharist shared by what was clearly a group with a sense of community.

For Ian and for others it is important that Moot is a new monastic community. The community has explored the Benedictine rule in terms of the way the community comes to decisions, the leader exercising a wide, inclusive consultative process in decision-making. People understand something of servant leadership and recognize that there is room for different vocations within the community. Ian is deeply committed to the new monastic language, though critical of the way it has been introduced (and too easily abandoned) else-where. He recognizes that what he is wanting to develop is, in some ways, more Franciscan than Benedictine.

Ian saw a long-term future for the kind of community Moot aspires to be and does not believe all emerging churches must necessarily remain small. He shares the view that the emerging churches will remain quite a small part of the mixed economy church and that their greatest contribution should be to re-energize the inherited church and not least its worship. Meanwhile Moot has produced six ordinands during its relatively short life, with three more entering the process.

12

Listen to what the Spirit is saying to the churches

The emergent churches that we visited were, in general, quite small. Some were the size of cell churches, meeting in homes, whether it was in an apartment in New York (Transmission) or in a house on the edge of Telford (Safe Space). Their membership was around 10 or 12. They did not have the aim to grow large, to move into a different sort of meeting place or to take on a different character. Others were larger. Transcendence in York was a gathering of 150 people, but Visions, the community that organizes the monthly Transcendence experience in York Minster, numbers only about 20 and has done through its nearly 20 years of existence. Blessèd in Gosport, meeting in St Thomas's Church, has a core community of five or six, though a particular event might attract as many as 70. Moot, meeting in a city church in London, numbers about 20.

There are larger communities, especially in the United States. The Crossing community numbers 50 to 60. The Church of the Apostles regularly has 80 to 100 on a Sunday. Thad's is unusual in functioning on a Sunday morning, more like the pattern of inherited church, and there were 150 people present on the Sunday we were there. But these were and are the exceptions. Emergent communities are generally small, expect to remain so and meet the needs of those who share their life precisely because they are small, intimate and highly participatory.

It follows from this that their most significant contribution to the life of the wider Church will not be to replace inherited churches, but to influence them. More and more small emergent churches may spring up, though some will have a short life (and emergent churches are unconcerned about that), and exist alongside the inherited churches. Sometimes they will develop healthy, mutually supportive relationships with them, especially if they are integrated into the life of the local diocese. Inevitably sometimes there will be some suspicion and sense of competition, though everyone should seek to overcome that. Emergent churches are not going to take over and the inherited churches disappear.

Instead the role of the emergent churches, and especially of the creative thinkers within them, is to influence the inherited churches, in the way that every movement of the Spirit has done. The evangelical movement of the eighteenth century, the Anglo-Catholic revival of the nineteenth century, the liturgical movement, the ecumenical movement and the charismatic movement of the twentieth century have all, in their different ways, changed and reshaped the experience of church for people who have never thought of themselves as embracing any of those movements. Fresh expressions and emergent churches will significantly renew churches of every kind, especially if those churches are ready to learn and eager to receive.

The first lesson the inherited churches may need to learn is a difficult and somewhat negative one. It is to understand the pain of those who have walked away because traditional churches seemed to exclude. 'I was not welcome there,' is something we frequently heard, 'I did not fit in.' There is an urgent need for the churches to look at just how inclusive they are. Most believe they are; few rejoice in exclusivity. Very few churches, for instance, would think of themselves as exclusive of the feminine, but, whether because they exclude women from ordained ministry or because of the language they use of men, or of God, often there is presented an over-masculine, paternal or patriarchal understanding of both the human and the divine. While exclusion of the feminine was not overtly articulated as a reason for a sense of exclusion from traditional churches, there is no doubt that emerging churches are more inclusive of the feminine.

The sense of exclusion of gay, lesbian, bisexual and transgender people is perhaps more obvious and, if we are honest, more difficult for the inherited churches, many of which struggle to come to terms with changes in attitudes in wider society that seem to them to challenge what they understand as the plain teaching of Scripture. But even a church that is actively struggling with the nature of sexuality, issues of Christian ethics and lifestyle can work at creating a sense of welcome and invitation to all for whom Christ died. Full inclusion does not have to wait for full agreement on what most delights the heart of God.

There is also, especially in the UK, a rather different sort of pain experienced by those who came to faith in evangelical churches of a conservative kind (more usually non-Anglican ones) and have since experienced that strand of Christianity, with its perceived emphasis on shame, guilt and sin, as narrow, untenable and harmful. In reacting against it, many have walked away from the church, but some have found a way back to faith through the emergent churches, where they sense a more generous orthodoxy. They feel able to ask questions within a framework of a broader theology and to be fully themselves in an environment that does not see everything exclusively in terms of personal salvation. 'Post-evangelicals' are to be found in quite large numbers among the leaders of emergent churches. We were repeatedly told about people who felt that they had been damaged by the pressures of trying to conform to the expectations of some conservative evangelical churches.

There is one other very large company of people who experience exclusion. It is a generational exclusion and a very wide one at that. Generation X (Gen X), as it has been called (usually understood as those born in the 1960s and 1970s), and even more Generation Y (Gen Y – those born since 1980), have often either had no experience of the church or, if they have, have been left puzzled by it or without any sense of how it might relate to their lives. Of course, in every city and in some towns and villages one can find church congregations with people under 50, and even under 20, highly engaged in the church's life; but in terms of the proportion of the population even the most 'successful' churches are reaching only a small minority. 'I don't go in for that church shit,' was the comment of the young woman who nevertheless walked up the hill each Sunday evening for Compline at St Mark's Cathedral in Seattle, and this is not untypical of the rejection as irrelevant or even unsavoury of much of traditional church life. If emergent churches can reach some of these alienated young people and challenge their sense of excluded generations, they will be doing the wider Church a huge service.

One of the key things we found about the emergent churches, common to them all, was their ability to create communities where people with very different views could live in harmony one with another. It would be wrong, for instance, to think that everybody in an emergent church holds to the view that gay and lesbian relationships are without problem for the Christian. There will be those in emergent churches who hold quite traditional views about sexuality. The very same emergent churches will have members who are in gay and lesbian relationships. Somehow the community holds. It is quite difficult to pinpoint exactly why. In part it is the acceptance of the postmodern assumption about the subjectivity of truth – in effect, 'what is true for me may not be true for you and I can live with that' – and that is something about which many in the institutional church will worry, for the objectivity of truth is something accepted without question. This easy coexistence is also a product of the small-ness of community. These are groups of people who give time to relationship, get to know each other well, listen to each other's stories, perhaps get to see the person as God sees them. These are communi-ties in which there is an intimacy and vulnerability that creates a culture of acceptance of people very different from ourselves.

Beyond that, these are communities of exploration. The emphasis on the Open Space, where people engage prayerfully with the relation-ship between Scripture and life, as a key part of worship, will always create an openness and provisionality that will never believe that the last word has been heard and so there is always opportunity to walk on together. The Open Space is a really significant part of most emergent church worship and a specifically liturgical expression of this acceptance and inclusivity.

Such mutual acceptance is not, of course, restricted to the emergent churches. Many church communities model that, but many others do not handle it well. When it comes to the life of the Church on a larger scale, whether the diocese, the national church or an interna-tional communion, it becomes harder and harder to live with that degree of tolerant inclusivity, but in the life of the small emergent churches we have a model for others to try to emulate.

In the course of our pilgrimage and in reflecting on it in this book, we have identified five important insights in relation to worship that the inherited churches need take seriously.

The first, and probably the most important, relates to the whole business of belonging, behaving and believing, that Phyllis Tickle explores so helpfully in *The Great Emergence*. It has its implication in relation to hospitality and the open table, powerfully exemplified by the liturgical arrangement at St Gregory of Nyssa in San Francisco, where you need to go round the altar table before you can reach the baptismal font.

Believing, behaving, belonging are all three important in Christian life. They do not always (perhaps not often in our culture) come neatly like that as three distinct elements of our lives, let alone in a sequence where we first come to believe, then are drawn into a Christian lifestyle and then through Baptism and Eucharist are incorporated into the community. They are all mixed in together and people experience them very differently. Some people find belonging first. They can belong to a church for a long time before they can say with real conviction that they believe. Belonging is often where they need to be before they can begin to have the space to explore belief. And belonging is often where they need to be even when they have not yet come to a point where their behaviour follows Christian norms. What God longs for is that through our Christian pilgrimage – a lifetime of journeying with Jesus – we will come to walk the Jesus way (behaving), to have faith in God who loves us unconditionally (believing) and to play our part in God's mission (belonging to Christ's Church and working for God's kingdom on earth). But it does not happen neatly and tidily; perhaps it is not meant to.

More and more in our society the church has understood the need for hospitality and welcome, something deeper and more sustained than the smile from the person giving out the hymn books at the church door. Just as few churches think of themselves as exclusive, few think of themselves as unwelcoming. But there is no doubt that many who try to cross the threshold do not experience a hospitable church and therefore are denied the chance to meet the hospitable God.

God is a hospitable, generous God, always inviting, always welcoming, always wanting to draw us in. What we found among the emergent churches was, more than anything else, an emphasis on sharing the hospitality of God in making churches communities of acceptance and invitation to be at home, to explore faith and to sense welcome. For the inherited churches, demonstrating the hospitality of God would begin with simple things like noticeboards that say 'Welcome' and give correct and inviting information, websites that are up to date and enticing. It involves not only the person at the door before a service who genuinely looks pleased to see the newcomer and is ready to help them, but some care through the service for those who might be a bit lost, worried or confused, service books and leaflets that make things easy, reassurance that the not-quite-silent toddler really is a delight and not a source of irritation, invitation to come to the altar when others do without too much concern about who is qualified to do so, introductions to people over coffee after the service, an invitation to return, and just sometimes, a willingness to listen while a life story pours out. If we put all that together it represents a generous, caring, hospitable community, behaving like that not simply because it wants more people in church on Sunday but because disciples of Jesus Christ want to mirror the hospitality of God, who is always inviting to the party. We saw a lot of that in the emergent churches.

In the middle of it lies a difficult question. If the invitation to the altar is about not having too much concern about who is qualified to come, what is happening to the long, almost unchallenged tradition of the church that the Eucharist is for the baptized? The emergent churches all have in common a fairly easy acceptance that belonging before believing leads to eucharistic participation before Baptism. Some of them simply accept that that is the way it is. Others proclaim it as an important insight and reversal of the tradition. In adopting such a policy, they are not on their own. On both sides of the Atlantic there are more churches than in the past that, at very least, are taking a more relaxed view on admission to Communion and in some cases issuing a strong invitation to all who receive.

Here, as has been mentioned before, the positions in the Church of England and in The Episcopal Church are different. In England the norm remains that admission to Communion follows not only from Baptism but also from Confirmation, normally administered after a candidate has reached the age of ten, but with widespread (but minority) provision for a bishop to allow admission of baptized children to Communion from a much earlier age without Confirmation. In addition the canons allow communicant members of other Christian churches (who will not have been episcopally confirmed) to receive Communion in Anglican churches. The majority of churches follow these conventions, often with a fairly complex instruction in service books about who may receive or who may receive a blessing at the time of the Distribution. The result at any eucharistic celebration is a great mix: some adults receive the consecrated bread and wine, others, sometimes quite a large number (some but not all of them baptized), receive a blessing; some quite young children receive the consecrated elements, some older children do not. It is an unsatisfactory and confused picture that needs attention. There will be a few churches – traditionally evangelical churches in touch with Free

Church practice – that follow a different approach and invite to the table 'all those who love the Lord Jesus'. This is a broader invitation than just to the baptized, but is probably not an all-inclusive invitation, such as to those who are exploring belonging before going very deeply into believing. At the present time, to add to the total picture, some churches have begun to invite all to come to receive the consecrated bread and wine, without any qualification – though the number of churches doing this is quite small. It is, after all, contrary to the canons.

In The Episcopal Church, the situation is less complex. Non-communicants coming to the altar for a blessing is fairly rare. Baptism is seen as sufficient qualification to be a communicant. Young children are, in many communities, admitted to Communion. Confirmation is no longer the gateway to communicant life. An Episcopalian visiting an English church will be very surprised by the number of non-communicants. In addition to that, the unofficial trend towards an open table, recognizing that some of those who come to receive are unbaptized, is more advanced and widespread than in England.

There has been little serious theological writing around this subject and, probably wisely, a reluctance to raise the issue in the councils of the Church, given that it could be another highly divisive matter in a Communion that has enough of such already. But there is something of a trend developing by stealth and the Church will need to address it. Among those who have thought this through, both sides can turn to Scripture for some support. Those advocating change will go to the Gospels and recall the stories of Jesus eating with others, sometimes in the intimacy of a household, sometimes in satisfying a huge crowd. There was no rubric about who might receive when Jesus took the loaves and fishes and provided a meal for 5,000! But are we to understand the feeding stories as sufficiently eucharistic that they suggest an open table for the Eucharist today? Clearly they have resonances of the Eucharist, not least because John puts his account of the feeding as the introduction to his teaching about Jesus as the bread of life. But the context is very different from the account of the Last Supper in the upper room where the evangelists, surprisingly perhaps, are insistent that the meal was with 'the twelve'. No mention of other disciples, not even the Lord's mother and the other women who were there next day at the foot of the cross and in the same upper room seven weeks later at Pentecost. There is no avoiding the fact that the Last Supper feels exclusive.

But it is Paul's theology that challenges more deeply the open table at which those still on a journey into Christian discipleship are welcome. Paul's understanding in 1 Corinthians 11 is that it is the body of Christ into which we were baptized that eats the bread that, at another level, is the body, and drinks the wine from the cup, that is the Christ's blood. And he adds that those who 'eat and drink without discerning the body, eat and drink judgement against themselves' (1 Corinthians 11.29).

It is difficult to make a strong case from Scripture for a change in practice, unless one falls back on a more general assertion that the God revealed in Jesus is always the inviting, welcoming, including God, who will always be on the side of those who want to abandon regulations and knock down barriers. Nor is it easy to see how such a long and (in the catholic tradition) unbroken rule can be lightly set aside. One has to ask why the church moved so quickly to a view that the Eucharist was only for the faithful. The practice came from a period of persecution, where knowing who was with you and who was against you was important. But was it only that or was there not a deeper theological conviction about the nature of the Body of Christ?

Perhaps the only overwhelming case for change lies in the fact that the church ministers in an extraordinarily different context from almost every generation that has gone before. In fact, the context of the time of Jesus as portrayed in the Gospels, with its picture of religious legalism, challenged by the abundant and shared grace known in Jesus, seems to mirror our own time, with the same stark contrast between the world of religion and the hunger for a nurtured spiritual life. The move from a model that sees belonging as emerging from believing to one that accepts the reverse is a major shift that calls for radical rethinking of how we 'do church', including how we initiate people into membership and how we celebrate the sacraments. It is only the fast-changing cultural context that can seriously challenge the way we have interpreted the biblical material and a tradition that goes back to the sub-apostolic age. Even in that context, there is a need for the church to be wary about 'spiritual tourism' – people simply experimenting with what feels good for them without a sense of serious searching or commitment. Eucharistic participation cannot be reduced to 'just being there to snack'.

For all the danger that it may sound like compromise, we need to celebrate a God whose sense of order does not extend to narrow prescription or to conditional grace. It may be the will of God for the Church that the Eucharist should be the ultimate expression of communion with the Trinity and with one another within the Body of Christ, but that does not prevent it being a means of grace for those who, on their way to faith, find themselves for a moment incorporated into something that they are not yet ready to commit to or meeting with One who they are not yet ready to embrace. The outcome of that may be a church that puts more emphasis on invitation than on qualification, but is also ready, by good teaching and gentle leading, to move people, who have stumbled into eucharistic participation without knowing its full significance, to the baptismal water and to a sense of being part of the Body. In other words, if they find themselves regularly at the table, they should learn very soon about the font.

The other four insights can be expressed more briefly. The first of the four is the strong commitment among the members of emergent churches to the discipline of liturgical planning and preparing. It was very striking to us that people wanted to express their commitment both to faith and to the community by participation in the preparation of worship. They were much more interested in that than necessarily having a particular and public role when the time for celebration actually arrived. This is very different from the experience of worshippers in the inherited churches, where most people arrive on a Sunday expecting worship to be provided for them by others. They may be content simply to be recipients, to allow something good to happen to them. They may want to express what is happening more dynamically – they are offering their worship to God, genuinely, highly engaged, but able to do so because others have done the hard work of preparing the liturgy. Or they may be clear that they want to express something about their membership of the Body by exercising a particular ministry – ringing bells, welcoming people, reading the Scriptures, leading prayers, being eucharistic ministers – but unless they are, for instance, a choir member or an instrumentalist, who will have practised and rehearsed, they will not have had major input into the planning and preparing. So they will not 'own' the liturgy in quite the same way as those who have met and given time and energy to the planning and preparing.

This is an area in which the members of emergent churches have something to teach. Worship for many of them is not what happens for an hour at the main weekly gathering. That is simply the out-working or the climax of a more costly involvement. It may have started in some study together of the Scriptures that are to be read (often working away at the lectionary choices even when they look difficult). It may have developed into an evening of shaping and planning. It may then have led to a good deal of time spent creating a prayer station or writing a song or thinking through the practicalities of a ritual. That is understood as participation as much as, and perhaps more than, what is contributed when everybody comes together. The result is a gathering where there is a deep level of commitment and engagement to the enterprise and to those who have helped to bring it into being.

It is not possible to produce such a pattern in most inherited church communities every week, and even in emergent churches the time commitment is sometimes such that they prepare in this way only fortnightly or monthly. Preparation of this kind is greedy of time. It assumes a greater variety of liturgical form than some communities would find helpful. It is only possible in small communities – a church of 200 could not involve everybody in the preparation, beyond perhaps in gathering for *lectio divina* in groups some time during the week. But there is more possibility of participation in planning and preparing than most of our churches find time for. It could be time well spent, and if even 25 per cent of the congregation were involved even once a month in preparing the weekly service, that could be transformative in terms of people having a richer experience of both the liturgy and the spiritual life.

The next insight relates quite closely to the previous one. It is the huge significance for most of the emergent churches of Open Space or Stations, which have been described at various points in this book, for they are significant in terms of participation in the community's life, in terms of engagement with Scripture and preaching, in terms of personal spiritual development and in terms of the experience of prayer.

In the inherited church context, the reading of the Scriptures leads into preaching by a single person, perhaps a very short period of silence and then the creed to express common faith, after which there are intercessory prayers often related only marginally, if at all, to what has gone before. The pattern we observed frequently in emergent churches was that the reading of the Scriptures leads to preaching or teaching by a single person, followed by either open discussion or contributions by a limited number of individuals. The exploration of the Scriptures and the exercise of relating them to contemporary issues and to the individual's faith journey continues in Open Space. This is usually in a series of stations around the room, with prayer (individual and personal) forming an important element in at least some of those stations.

The use of such stations is developing in worship in the inherited churches, not often in the Sunday Eucharist but on other liturgical occasions, and it has much to commend it. Indeed, more generally, an approach to the exploration of Scripture that involves some engagement in discussion with the preacher in the liturgy, as well as the breaking out into Open Space to take the engagement further and make it more personally applicable, must be good and something more churches should embrace. However good the preaching of one person and however much we need to retain confidence in sermons as a proper and effective means of conveying Christian truth, there need to be other ways in which people can appropriate the Scriptures and relate them to their lives. Although it is good that people gather on weekday nights in house groups for Bible study, there is sometimes a need both to bring that into the main act of worship in the week and also to make it accessible in a variety of ways to people at very different stages of their faith development and at very different stages of their lives. The advantage of the series of stations is that people can be drawn to something that looks as if it might speak to their particular need or condition. If they are right, they have found treasure. If they are wrong, they can move on and try another station.

The convention in many emergent churches that the primary focus in Open Space is to move the explorer/worshipper into prayer is also a good one. In the Eucharist in traditional church life, intercession is very often almost unconnected with the rest of the liturgy and rarely touches the soul. The prayer the individual prays arises much more from the exploration and engages them on a more profound level.

There is a downside to such an approach. The individual could always choose a station that appealed because it seemed to engage with a comfortable area, rather than a challenging one. For example, the prayer might always be too much about the individual's own need and never break out in intercession for the world. But it is worth developing a model of Open Space that avoids these pitfalls. What helps is the eucharistic setting, which most of the emergent churches we visited thought important. For each person, having explored in their own way at their own level with their own concerns, is then brought back to the group, gathering around the altar table, the individual drawn into the communal, where intercession can range broadly. By participation in the eucharistic action (as, for instance, at The Crossing with the shared gestures), each worshipper can sense the belonging to Christ and to one another that the Eucharist celebrates.

The penultimate insight for the inherited churches is the question of the return to liturgical complexity, discussed at the beginning of Chapter 9. It is a very fundamental challenge for churches that have put much energy in the last couple of generations to the simplifying and streamlining of the liturgy in order to make it more accessible and its signs and symbols more effective. If Karen Ward and those who share her view are right, then such simplicity can only work in a place where there is a highly developed shared mono-culture. The reality is that we live in a world where in nearly every community there are many cultures, many experiences of the spiritual, many variations of human need. The more diverse the community, the more we need to offer different ways to explore the mystery of God and indeed the mystery of the individual's own being. This is another reason for valuing the insights of the Open Space approach. It is a recognition that we need to employ every sense, many insights and a variety of actions and gestures if we are to find the one thing that will start people on their pilgrimage or refresh them on the way. Liturgy needs to have sufficient complexity, to be sufficiently multi-layered, that people gathered in one community may experience God diversely.

We see it happening already in many inherited church settings. Churches that used to be uninterested in icons, in candles, in chants and prayer beads, increasingly recognize that we need to employ a variety of different phenomena, artefacts and styles of prayer if we are to help people to connect to the divine and to discover their true selves. The emergent churches are an encouragement to do this and provide some creative ideas and examples of good practice about how it may be done.

Part of this return to complexity is a renewed willingness to bring 'out of his treasure what is new and what is old' (Matthew 13.52). It means, on the one hand, being willing to pack away words, songs, ceremonies and approaches to worship that do not, in this generation or in a particular community, seem to connect people to God. That always needs to be done with humility, recognizing that what does not seem to connect here and now has done so in the past, and possibly will again. So it needs to stay in the treasure house, waiting for its day to come again, but not to be slavishly used where its impact has been lost, at least for the time being. Such humility is not difficult to acquire when one observes how other things, which our forebears or even ourselves have packed away as no longer appropriate, suddenly look to be useful tools again. Some of the things we have jettisoned – the prayer we thought archaic, the painting we thought unfashionable, the symbolic action that seemed obscure – future generations will recover. Sometimes the recovery need not wait for a future generation – on occasions we will need to look again at some of the texts and customs we have too hastily set aside. The extraordinary thing is that some of the good things from the treasure house of tradition that the emergent churches can receive from the inherited church – pilgrimage, fasting, the liturgical cycle – are treasures they are in fact seizing and developing with more commitment and creativity than the inherited church from which they are receiving them. 'Look to the rock from which you were hewn' (Isaiah 51.1), the emergent churches seem to be saying to the inherited churches; 'you have the treasure house and the opportunity to bring out the treasures and enrich the Church with a beautiful complexity that can draw in people with all their diversity.'

Finally, among the insights from the emergent churches, is the desire to explore what is sometimes called 'the new monasticism'. Some communities, such as Moot and the Church of the Apostles, are very determined on the establishment of a community, if possible living under one roof (as COTA has at Fremont Abbey), or at very least with a daily gathering for prayer (St Gregory of Nyssa has had that strongly established over many years) and with members adopting a 'rule of life', though not always called that. For some the term 'rhythm of life' is more appealing, but whatever the name, the key to it is mutual commitment, disciplined prayer life and social action. At a time when the conventional religious life in the West, in Anglicanism as in the Roman Catholic Church, has been experiencing a crisis in vocations and some loss of direction and identity, it is in the emergent churches that some of the most creative thinking has come about how community life might be given fresh expression for the twenty-first century, drawing on the old monastic wisdom, but appropriate to today's world. Again, the movement is mirrored in the inherited churches by those exploring the idea of religious orders in a new way that is not restricted to the emergent churches. But it must be an encouragement to those looking for new ways to live the religious life in the inherited churches that new emergent churches can see the need for such communities to provide spiritual stability for individuals and for the movement.

These are the liturgical gifts that the emergent churches can give to the wider Church. They are, of course, in several cases the giving back of something that comes from the inherited church and from the centuries-old Christian traditions. And that is perhaps a clue to the greatest gift that these fresh expressions of church can give to the rest of us. The greatest gift is to continue to occupy the space we do, but with renewed confidence. There are things we need to change and there are things we need to abandon (at least for a season), but there is so much good, so much wisdom and so much of God in the church. Somehow we have allowed ourselves to lose confidence in it. That loss of confidence is in some places a very deep one. For it has become a loss of confidence not only in the kind of liturgy we offer but in ourselves and even in God. We have allowed ourselves to doubt whether the Holy Spirit will fill our worship, whether God really will 'pitch his tent' among us when we celebrate the liturgy, whether Jesus Christ can really be encountered in the breaking open of the Scriptures and the breaking of the bread. It is exciting to sense in the emergent churches such a level of confidence, commitment, enthusiasm and expectation.

Their greatest gift is not to copy their every idea, as if it would translate into the different circumstances of our worship week by week, but to recover their sense of confidence in what we have been given and its potential to draw us and others more effectively into the experience of the love and beauty and holiness of God. Such confidence will make us more creative and more adventurous in our worship and will allow the grace of God to be experienced both in the traditional things we shall do better and in the new things that we shall do well. And if and when that happens, for all that the emergent churches are few and small and may remain so, we shall want to honour them for the part they will have played in our renewal.

Appendix
Church communities described in this book

———————•◦•———————

Blesséd began in 2004. It now meets in St Thomas' Parish Church, Gosport, UK. The Reverend Simon Rundell is its priest. Worship is monthly and attendance may vary from as few as 20 to as many as 70. <www.blessed.org.uk>

Ethos @ St Nick's began in 2007 and meets every other month at St Nicholas' Parish Church, Portsmouth, UK. It is designed for those outside the church or those with a negative experience of the church and attracts about 35 of a wide age range. The Reverend Bev Robertson is their priest. <www.ethos-altworship.blogspot.com>

Home is a fresh expression church in Oxford, UK, sponsored initially by the Anglican Diocese of Oxford. Its average weekly attendance is approximately 30 people. It currently meets in St Mary's and St John's Church. The Reverend Matt Rees is their priest. <www.home-online. org>

Moot was founded in 2003 in the diocese of London by the Reverend Ian Mobsby. The congregation describes itself as neo-monastic, with participants mainly aged 30s to 40s. They currently meet in various locations and worship attendance is generally around 20 people. <www. moot.uk.net>

Safe Space was started in 2006, meeting in the home of Mark Berry, the 'guardian' of the community, in Telford, UK. The core community is about 10, with members aged between 20 and 40. <www.smallfire.org/safe spacepage1.html>

St Gregory of Nyssa is a San Francisco parish of The Episcopal Church and not technically an emerging church. It was founded in 1978 by the Reverends Paul Fabian and Donald Schell. The current rector is the Reverend Paul Fromberg. There are approximately 300 members. <www. stgregorys.org>

St Mark's Cathedral Seattle is the cathedral of the Episcopal Diocese of Olympia. Traditional in most of its worship, it has for many years attracted to a weekly Compline service 500 people in their 20s. <www. saintmarks.org>

St Paul's Church Seattle is a progressive Anglo-Catholic parish of The Episcopal Church, with a membership of approximately 250. The rector is the Reverend Melissa Skelton. <www.stpaulseattle.org>

Sanctus1 is an Anglican/Methodist sponsored fresh expression, meeting in Nexus, an arts centre/café, in a Methodist complex in Manchester, UK. The Reverend Al Lowe, a Methodist minister, is the leader of Sanctus1. It meets twice weekly, with attendees in the 20 to 40 age range. <www. sanctus1.co.uk>

Thad's is a preaching station of the Episcopal Diocese of Los Angeles. It began in 2006 and is pastored by the Reverend Jimmy Bartz. The congregation of approximately 150 members meets currently in a Jewish synagogue on the west side of Los Angeles. <www.thads.org>

The Church of the Apostles is an Episcopal/Lutheran congregation founded in 2002 and now residing in the Fremont area of Seattle. Its community building is styled 'Fremont Abbey'. The community is led by the Reverend Karen Ward. It has an average weekly attendance of between 80 and 100. <www.apostleschurch.org>

The Crossing was founded in 2005 and is a weekday congregation of St Paul's Episcopal Cathedral in Boston, Massachusetts. The average attendance at its worship is 50. It is led by the Reverend Stephanie Spellers. <www.thecrossingboston.org>

Transcendence is an offshoot of Visions, a fresh expression community that has existed in York, UK, since 1992. Visions is a weekly gathering of about 20 people in St Cuthbert's Church. Transcendence is a monthly worship event in York Minster, organised by Visions, attracting up to 200 people. Until summer 2010 both were led by the Reverend Sue Wallace. <www.transcendenceyork.org>

Transmission is a 'house church' meeting in Manhattan, New York, since 2006. Transmission is not affiliated to any denomination. It is a small group of about 10, in their late 20s to 30s, with some members over 40. It was founded by Isaac Everett, who is still its leader, and Bowie Snodgrass, who is still associated with it. <www.transmission.org>

Copyright acknowledgements

The publisher and authors acknowledge with thanks permission to reproduce extracts from the following. Every effort has been made to seek permission to use copyright material reproduced in this book. The publisher apologizes for those cases where permission might not have been sought and, if notified, will formally seek permission at the earliest opportunity.

'Come, all you who thirst', Mike Riddell, published in 'Bread and Wine, Beer and Pies', in Pete Ward, *Mass Culture: The Interface of Eucharist and Mission*, Abingdon, Bible Reading Fellowship, 2008, reproduced with permission.

'All are invited, all are included', Jonny Baker, *Spirit of the New* album, <www.proost.co.uk>, reproduced with permission.

'Like a woman looking for treasure lost' and 'You say you know the face of God?', Beverley Robertson, Ethos @ St Nick's, used with permission.

Compline at St Mark's Cathedral, Seattle, used with permission.

Life Together in the Way of Jesus, A Rule of Life for the Church of the Apostles, used with permission, <www.apostleschurch.org>.

'The Great Thanksgiving Prayer of Cain Our Father', the Revd Richard Fabian, founder of St Gregory of Nyssa Episcopal Church, San Francisco, used with permission.

'We meet in the name', Ian Mobsby, used with permission.

'God of all mercy', *Enriching our Worship*, Church House Publishing, 1998, p. 56.

'We gather with one another and with you', Quinton Peeples, used with permission.

Extracts from Ian Mobsby, *New Monastic Friars*, Paraclete Press, forthcoming, used with permission.

'You are God's servants gifted with dreams and visions', Diane Karay Tripp, used with permission.

'Get up', Ian Mobsby, used with permission.

'The liturgy after the liturgy', Mark Berry, used with permission.

'Broken', words and music by Tara Ward, inspired by Henri Nouwen, recorded at the Church of the Beloved, Edmonds, Washington, <www.BelovedsChurch.org>, used with permission.

'Given', words and music by Tara Ward and Ryan Marsh, inspired by Henri Nouwen, recorded at the Church of the Beloved, Edmonds, Washington, <www.BelovedsChurch.org>, used with permission.

'Cradle it, and let its hard exterior', Simon Rundell, used with permission.

'40 days', Hunter Perrin, used with permission.

'Prayer of invocation' and 'Closing prayer', Church of the Apostles, Seattle, WA, <www.apostleschurch.org>, used with permission.

'God of unchangeable power and eternal light', *Common Worship: Daily Prayer*, Church House Publishing, 2005. *Common Worship: Daily Prayer* is copyright © The Archbishops' Council, 2005, and extracts are reproduced by permission.

'God of all the nations upon the earth', The Book of Common Prayer with the Additions and Deviations proposed in 1928, copyright © Oxford University Press.

'God of all the nations of the earth', The Book of Common Prayer, 1979 of The Episcopal Church, Church Hymnal Corporation and the Seabury Press, p. 206.

'Ever living God', The Book of Common Prayer, 1979 of The Episcopal Church, Church Hymnal Corporation and the Seabury Press, p. 816.

'Almighty God, who called your Church', *Common Worship: Festivals*, Church House Publishing, 2008, p. 342. *Common Worship: Festivals* is copyright © The Archbishops' Council, 2008, and extracts are reproduced by permission.

References

Mark Berry, *Navigatio: Pocket Liturgies from Safe Space*, Telford, Proost, 2007.

Common Worship: Ordination Services, London, Church House Publishing, 2007.

'Dancing with God' DVD, St Gregory of Nyssa Episcopal Church, San Francisco, 2000.

Isaac Everett, *The Emergent Psalter*, Harrisburg, PA, Church Publishing, 2009.

Tim Keel, *Intuitive Leadership*, Grand Rapids, MI, Emersion Books, 2007, p. 177.

Brian McLaren, *A Generous Orthodoxy*, Grand Rapids, MI, Zondervan, 2004, p. 236.

Brian McLaren, *Finding our Way: The Return of the Ancient Practice*, Nashville, Thomas Nelson, 2008, pp. 21–8.

Ian Mobsby, *New Monastic Friars*, Orleans, MA, Paraclete Press, 2011.

Gerald Priestland, *Priestland's Progress: One Man's Search for Christianity Now*, London, BBC Publications, 1981, p. 59.

Peter Rollins, *How (Not) to Speak of God*, Orleans, MA, Paraclete Press, 2006. pp. 42, 56.

Steven Shakespeare, *Prayers for an Inclusive Church*, Norwich, Canterbury Press, 2008.

Bryan Spinks, *The Worship Mall*, London, SPCK, 2010.

Phyllis Tickle, *The Great Emergence*, Grand Rapids, MI, Baker Books, 2008, pp. 149, 150–1, 152, 159.